Proclaiming
the Good News

Books in the Stephen Olford
Biblical Preaching Library

Believing Our Beliefs
Biblical Answers to Personal Problems
Committed to Christ and His Church
Fresh Lessons from Former Leaders
Inviting People to Christ
Living Words and Loving Deeds
The Pulpit and the Christian Calendar 1
The Pulpit and the Christian Calendar 2
The Pulpit and the Christian Calendar 3

Proclaiming the Good News

Evangelistic Expository Messages

Stephen F. Olford

Baker Books

A Division of Baker Book House Co
Grand Rapids, Michigan 49516

© 1998 by Stephen F. Olford

Published by Baker Books
a division of Baker Book House Company
P.O. Box 6287, Grand Rapids, MI 49516-6287

Printed in the United States of America

ISBN 0-8010-9061-X

Scripture quotations are taken from the New King James Version. Copyright © 1979, 1980, 1982 by Thomas Nelson, Inc., Publishers. Used by permission. All rights reserved.

For current information about all releases from Baker Book House, visit our web site:

http://www.bakerbooks.com

Contents

Grateful Acknowledgments   7

Introduction   9

1. Saved by Grace through Faith (Joshua 2:1–22; 6:16–17, 22–26; Matthew 1:1–6; Hebrews 11:31–33)   11
2. The Blood of Christ (Hebrews 12:22–25; 1 Peter 1:18–21; 1 John 1:5–10)   19
3. Radical Repentance (Luke 12:54–13:9)   28
4. Justification by Faith (Romans 3:19–31)   36
5. The Miracle of Conversion (Matthew 18:1–6)   44
6. The Overtures of the Gospel (Matthew 11:20–30)   50
7. The Story of Your Life (Matthew 21:33–46)   58
8. Salvation for a Call (Romans 10:11–17)   66
9. The Fears That Keep Us from Christ (Luke 8:26–39)   73
10. The Indwelt Life (Colossians 1:25–29)   81
11. Guarded by God (1 Peter 1:1–9)   87
12. Spiritual Unpreparedness (Matthew 25:1–13)   97
13. Man's Priceless Treasure (Mark 8:34–38)   104

Notes   115

Grateful Acknowledgments

The expository outlines of evangelistic sermons in this book are the finished product of messages delivered extemporaneously to Crusade audiences around the world and in the churches I have served. In the "flow" of such preaching, many quotes, concepts, and illustrations were brought to mind without specific documentation. I, therefore, acknowledge gratefully all sources of such material—heard or read—from the "gifts to men" (Eph. 4:8) with which our risen Lord has enriched the church.

Stephen F. Olford

Introduction

Preach the word. . . . *Do* the work of an evangelist" (2 Tim. 4:2, 5, italics mine). These two imperatives are as relevant today as when the great apostle Paul first dictated them. Even if a pastor/preacher does not consider himself an evangelist in the sense in which Philip was gifted (Acts 21:8), he is still mandated to "do the work of an evangelist." To "reach the people and preach the gospel," is our duty to God and our debt to humanity—in the local church and in the global ministry.

The evangelistic expositions offered in this first volume of two (volume 2 is titled *Inviting People to Christ*) are messages I actually preached at our evening "Witness" service at Calvary Baptist Church in New York City, and God was graciously pleased to bless them to the salvation of souls. Now it's your turn!

The Subjects. These are varied but *vital* in substance and scope. In adopting and adapting these subjects for your own preaching ministry, you may want to change titles and, therefore, modify structure. By all means do this—as long as you *are true to the text!*

The Sermons. Even though the thirteen sermons are individual messages, each one is an *exposition.* Whether in the churches I served in the U.K., or at Calvary Baptist Church in New York, or during crusades around the world, I have *never* preached an evangelistic sermon that was *not expository.* God has not promised to bless what *we* say, but He has promised to bless what He has forever said in His Son and in His Word.

The sermons do not constitute a series per se nor are they individual *topical* sermons. Each message is an expository treatment of a gospel theme—with its own call to decision. For this reason, there is no designed sequence that you need to follow.

The Spirit. Paul reminds us that "the letter kills, but the Spirit gives life" (2 Cor. 3:6). Words, *in and of themselves,* cannot produce the fruits of righteousness in the lives of those to whom we minister, even though they may be divine oracles. There has to be the vitalizing Spirit to charge the words with life-transforming power. The apostle states this clearly when writing to the Thessalonians. Mark his language: "Our gospel did not come to you *in word only,* but also in power, and in the Holy Spirit" (1 Thess. 1:5, italics mine). So as you expound these evangelistic sermons, make sure that you claim "the Promise of [the] Father"—even the endowment "with power from on high" (Luke 24:49).

Blessings on you as you preach!

1

Saved by Grace through Faith

Joshua 2:1–22; 6:16–17, 22–26; Matthew 1:1–6; Hebrews 11:31–33

By faith the harlot Rahab did not perish with those who did not believe, when she had received the spies with peace.

Hebrews 11:31

Introduction

The story of Rahab, the harlot, is one of the most remarkable narratives in Scripture. From the human standpoint this story teaches us something of the baseness of human nature, for Rahab was certainly an exceptionally evil character, and would present, apart from divine intervention, a hardened, inaccessible, hopeless case. But from the divine standpoint, the story of this debased woman teaches how wondrously grace superabounds where sin abounds and how God can save through a faith that is reasonable, relevant, and responsive. See in the first place how God, in grace, saves through:

I. A Reasonable Faith

"For we have heard how the LORD dried up the water of
the Red Sea for you when you came out of Egypt, and what
you did to the two kings of the Amorites who were on the
other side of the Jordan, Sihon and Og, whom you utterly
destroyed" (Josh. 2:10). By this we mean a faith which comes
through:

A. The Appreciation of Certain Facts

"We have *heard* how the LORD dried up the water of
the Red Sea for you when you came out of Egypt, and
what you did to the two kings of the Amorites who were
on the other side of the Jordan, Sihon and Og, whom you
utterly destroyed." Rahab appreciated:

1. HOW GOD DELIVERED HIS PEOPLE

When the Israelites were delivered from Egypt,
Rahab saw the love of God manifested toward a people who were in bondage, a love that did not rest until
it had provided a deliverer to emancipate the children
of Israel from the thralldom of Egypt.

2. HOW GOD DRIED UP THE RED SEA

She recognized the power of God, which defeated
enemies and swept aside every barrier to the progress
of the Canaan-bound pilgrims.

3. HOW GOD DESTROYED THE ENEMIES OF HIS PEOPLE

She appreciated God's righteousness and judgment,
for Sihon and Og, who represent the power and far-
reaching effects of sin, were utterly destroyed. These
were facts that she *heard,* and the Word of God tells
us that "faith comes by hearing, and hearing by the
word of God" (Rom. 10:17).

So a reasonable faith in this dark woman's heart found
its origin through the hearing of facts. In a like manner,

every sinner who seriously considers the wondrous facts of the gospel message will become the possessor of a reasonable faith that is necessary before God can save.

This reasonable faith also comes through:

B. An Acceptance of Certain Facts

"I know that the LORD has given you the land" (Josh. 2:9). Here we see the acceptance of the facts that Rahab had heard. Faith accepted all that God had done. She believed with all her heart that God, in love, would deliver all who trusted in Him and that in righteous judgment, He would utterly destroy all who deliberately disobeyed Him.

Such reasonable faith finally comes through:

C. An Acknowledgment of Certain Facts

"The LORD your God, He is God in heaven above and on earth beneath" (Josh. 2:11). Here was an acceptance and acknowledgment of faith. She not only believed the promises of God, but also believed the God of the promises.

Illustration

C. H. Spurgeon used this story to illustrate faith. A child is trapped in an upper level of a burning building. A strong man standing beneath the window where the child is crying calls up: "Jump! Drop into my arms!" Then Spurgeon observed: "It is a part of faith to know that there is a man there; still another part of faith to believe him to be a strong man; but the essence of faith is in trusting him fully and dropping into his arms." So it is with the sinner and the Savior.[1]

Let me point out that the faith-begetting facts for today are the very same facts that Rahab heard. They are:

1. THE FACT OF GOD'S LOVE

God, in love, has provided a means of salvation from the effects and power of sin. The great antitype of the Lord Jesus, the Savior of sinners, is Moses. "This is a

faithful saying and worthy of all acceptance, that Christ
Jesus came into the world to save sinners" (1 Tim. 1:15).

2. THE FACT OF GOD'S POWER

God has manifested his power in providing a new
living way to the land of promise. "Jesus said to him, 'I
am the way'" (John 14:6).

3. THE FACT OF GOD'S RIGHTEOUSNESS

God, in righteousness, has decreed judgment on all
sin. "[God] has appointed a day on which He will judge
the world in righteousness" (Acts 17:31).

Have you appreciated these facts? Have you accepted
them, made them your very own? Are you ready to acknowledge them as facts that you really believe?

In the second place, God in grace saves through:

II. A Relevant Faith

"Now therefore, I beg you, swear to me by the LORD, since
I have shown you kindness, that you also will show kindness to my father's house, and give me a true token" (Josh.
2:12). By this we see faith that relates divine grace to human
need. This is just what Rahab did. She realized her des-
perate need and that the visit of the spies was her opportunity to have that need met. "Now therefore, I beg you . . .
give me a true token." Careful consideration of each of these
words shows us the relevance of faith to our needs:

A. A Pressing Need

Rahab knew that there was no time to be lost and said,
"Now therefore, I beg you." She realized that Jericho was
a doomed city, on the ground of divine judgment, and
that very soon Jehovah's marching hosts would utterly
destroy both city and people. So she made no delay in

asking for a true token that would assure her safety in the coming day of wrath.

If only you knew how close the day of wrath is to you, you too would relate God's grace to your need. "Do not boast about tomorrow" (Prov. 27:1). "Behold, now is the accepted time; behold, now is the day of salvation" (2 Cor. 6:2 KJV).

Illustration

A lady received a summons that required her to appear in court on a certain day to answer a charge brought against her. She intended to secure a fine lawyer recommended to her by a close friend. However, she procrastinated until the court date was just a few days away. At last she contacted the attorney and asked him to defend her. Regretfully he replied: "Madam, had you called me last week I should gladly have represented you. However, several days ago I was appointed your judge!" The Lord Jesus Christ offers now to be the advocate of anyone who believes on Him. However, the day is coming when He will become the "judge [of] the living and the dead" (2 Tim. 4:1).[2]

We see again the relevance of faith to:

B. A Personal Need

"Now therefore, I beg you . . . give me." Rahab made a personal application for this true token of salvation. She was conscious of her personal need and was determined that she would have that need met.

Finally, we see the relevance of faith to:

C. A Practical Need

Rahab asks for something practical and real. "Give me," she said, "a true token." And she was provided immediately with a practical and sure way of salvation. She was told to tie a scarlet cord in the window.

Salvation today is equally as practical and sure. The Lord Jesus is the "scarlet cord," dyed with the blood of

His sacrifice. He is a "true token," a real living person, a Savior who has qualified by His death, burial, and resurrection to meet your every need and save you completely. You have the opportunity of proving Him to be real, vital, and practical in your salvation now.

In the third instance, God in grace saves through:

III. A Responsive Faith

"'According to your words, so be it.' And she sent them away, and they departed. And she bound the scarlet cord in the window" (Josh. 2:21). Rahab bound a scarlet cord in the window. It was a response that was:

A. Speedy

"She sent [the spies] away, and they departed." There was no time to delay. The spies had no sooner gone than she tied the cord in the window. Would to God that the response of your faith would be as speedy right now!

B. Sincere

"According to your words, so be it." Believing the testimony of the spies (God's servants), she was assured of deliverance in the coming day of wrath. The precious blood of the Lord Jesus Christ and the testimony of the Scriptures concerning its power are the outward tokens that bring assurance of salvation to the heart that trusts Christ.

C. Simple

"She bound the scarlet cord in the window." This was a simple act of faith. A child could have done this. This is why Jesus said, "Unless you are converted and become as little children, you will by no means enter the kingdom of heaven" (Matt. 18:3). Man complicates, but God simplifies!

Illustration

A boy was trying to comfort his younger brother who was dying and afraid. He told him to trust in Jesus. "What does that mean? What shall I do?" the frightened child asked. "Pray to Him!" the older boy replied. "I don't know how," cried the child. "Then just raise your hand. Jesus will know what you mean," the older brother urged. Great theologians could not improve on that uplifted hand as a beautiful illustration of the simplicity of faith.[3]

There was nothing complicated about tying a scarlet cord in the window. As we have observed, a child could do this. But it was God's way, and He saved her. In that grand word *saved,* I include the whole sweep of God's work in grace, for Rahab was granted:

1. SALVATION

"She bound the scarlet cord in the window." Although a vile sinner under the sentence of death, Rahab was saved the moment she tied the red cord in the window. Remember that if you want the scarlet cord of salvation to float from the window of your heart, you must trust Christ now.

2. SONSHIP

If you look at Matthew 1:5–6 ("Salmon begot Boaz by Rahab, Boaz begot Obed by Ruth, Obed begot Jesse, and Jesse begot David the king"), you will see that Rahab was received into the royal family! This could be true of you if you respond to the gospel; for the Word says, "As many as received Him, to them He gave the right to become children of God, to those who believe in His name" (John 1:12).

3. SERVICE

"What more shall I say? For the time would fail me to tell of [those] . . . who through faith subdued kingdoms, worked righteousness, obtained promises" (Heb. 11:32–33). In a very real sense, Rahab was used to bring Christ into the world! Do you want to have a life of true purpose in service? Find it in Christ, as you give Him the whole response of your faith.

Conclusion

If there is anyone who lightly regards the matters we have been considering, remember that the multitudes of Jericho fell and perished because of one sin in particular. You will find that sin recorded in connection with this story in Hebrews 11:31. It was the sin of unbelief. That which distinguished Rahab from the rest of the people of Jericho was not her superior morality, not her higher intelligence, nor her more exemplary character, for it appears that she was devoid of these qualities. It was rather her reasonable, relevant, and responsive faith in God's "true token." Because she believed, she was saved; because the rest disbelieved, they perished. Make this your response:

> Jesus, I do trust Thee,
> Trust without a doubt;
> Whosoever cometh,
> Thou wilt not cast out:
> Faithful is Thy promise,
> Precious is Thy blood:
> These my soul's salvation,
> Thou my Savior God!
>
> Mary Walker

The Blood of Christ

Hebrews 12:22–25; 1 Peter 1:18–21;
1 John 1:5–10

Knowing that you were not redeemed with corruptible
things, like silver or gold, . . . but with the precious blood
of Christ.

1 Peter 1:18–19

The blood of Jesus Christ His Son cleanses us from all sin.

1 John 1:7

Jesus . . . and to the blood of sprinkling that speaks better
things than that of Abel. See that you do not refuse Him
who speaks.

Hebrews 12:24–25

Introduction

Here is a subject that holds a place in the Bible like no
other. From Genesis to Revelation, we have the theme of the
blood of Christ. In the Old Testament it is prefigured; in the
New it is personified. J. H. Jowett used to say: "The only

authorized Alpine rope has a red worsted strand running through it from end to end; and the true followers of the Lord Jesus are known by their red strand, the blood sign." For our consideration of this subject, we are going to restrict ourselves to three passages in the New Testament. The first speaks of:

I. The Value of the Blood of Christ

"You were not redeemed with corruptible things, like silver or gold . . . but with the precious blood of Christ" (1 Peter 1:18–19). The writer speaks of the value of the blood of Christ as being incomparable, indispensable, and infinite.

A. Incomparable

"You were not redeemed with corruptible things, like silver or gold, . . . but with the precious blood of Christ." With carefully chosen language, the apostle Peter selects the two metals that were known for their high purchasing power as being totally incomparable to the value of the precious blood of Christ. What a word this is to the materialistic age in which we live! We are almost tempted to believe that we can buy our way into heaven with the "almighty" dollar. With the same outlook and spirit of the age, others imagine that they can merit salvation in terms of their good works, respectability, or generosity to the church. But Peter sweeps this all aside and affirms that only the blood of Christ can redeem.

B. Indispensable

"You were not redeemed with corruptible things, like silver or gold, . . . *but* with the precious blood of Christ." The author of Hebrews supports this with words borrowed from the Old Testament: "Without shedding of blood there is no remission" (Heb. 9:22). Although this doctrine of the most precious blood of Christ has been scandalized by the higher critics and by others who have blasphemously referred to this teaching as "the gospel of the slaughter-house," the message of the Bible remains the same. "Without shedding of blood there is no remission."

Illustration

Some years ago the American Associates of Blood Banks honored a man named Joe Kerkofsky as America's blood donor champion. Because he had lost an arm in an accident when he was six, Kerkofsky was rejected for military service in World War II. Since that time he had donated 31 gallons of blood. That is 20 times the amount of blood in a human body (10–12 pints). He had donated blood 250 times! Of his record Kerkofsky said: "Money can't buy the joy of giving blood to someone in need. It is contributing life itself." As remarkable as this story is, God Himself calls the shed blood of Christ "precious" in His sight.[1]

C. Infinite

"You were not redeemed with corruptible things, like silver or gold, . . . but with the precious blood of Christ, as of a lamb without blemish and without spot" (1 Peter 1:18–19). In this figure of speech, the apostle Peter sums up the infinite value of the precious blood of Christ in terms of:

1. THE SAVIOR'S SACRIFICIAL CHARACTER

"A lamb" reminds us of the words of Isaiah 53:7 where the prophet foretells that the Savior would be "led as a lamb to the slaughter, and as a sheep before its shearers is silent, so He opened not His mouth." The supreme submissiveness of our Lord Jesus Christ, even to death, is one of the great features of the doctrine of his redemptive work. There was no force or compulsion that led him to lay down his life, save that of his infinite love to his Father and needy mankind. He could say, "No one takes it from Me, but I lay it down of Myself. I have power to lay it down, and I have power to take it again. This command I have received from My Father" (John 10:18).

2. The Savior's Sinless Character

Christ is "a lamb without blemish." Let us remember that in the realm of His *conscience,* Christ "knew no sin" (2 Cor. 5:21). In the realm of His *character,* we read, "In Him there is no sin" (1 John 3:5). While in the realm of His *conduct,* we are told that He "committed no sin, nor was guile found in His mouth" (1 Peter 2:22). It is this sinlessness of the Lord Jesus that gives infinite value to the blood He shed on Calvary's tree.

3. The Savior's Stainless Character

Christ is "a lamb without blemish." No man can atone for his own sin, for every man is a depraved creature. Sin has invaded every part of his personality. Therefore, he must perish. "The wages of sin is death" (Rom. 6:23). And again: "The soul who sins shall die" (Ezek. 18:4). By this same token, no man can die for anyone else's sin. If the human race is to be redeemed, then nothing less than a sacrificial, sinless, and stainless life must be laid down.

As the Lamb of God on the cross, Jesus bore the sin of the world. As the Lamb on the throne, Jesus lives to save and to keep all who come to God by Him. "Therefore He is also able to save to the uttermost those who come to God through Him, since He ever lives to make intercession for them" (Heb. 7:25). How this should stir our hearts with wonder, love, and praise!

The next Scripture to which I wish to draw your attention speaks not so much of the value of the blood of Christ, as its virtue:

II. The Virtue of the Blood of Christ

Divine record states that "The blood of Jesus Christ His Son cleanses us from all sin" (1 John 1:7). That is to say, in the precious blood of Christ, which signifies the laying down of His life in the cruel and crucial death of the cross, there is virtue, or power, to deal with *every* form of sin. In this precious blood:

A. There Is Power to Deal with the Enslavement of Sin

"Whoever commits sin is a slave of sin" (John 8:34). By nature and by practice, men and women are enslaved by sin. Sin may take the form of uncontrolled temper, unbroken pride, or unmastered vice, but thank God, the power of the blood can redeem a man or woman from the slave market of sin. "We have redemption through His blood" (Eph. 1:7).

This redeeming power of the blood is now available because Christ has suffered *the price of sin*. The price that He paid, in terms of His lifeblood, was the cost of forfeited freedom. God allowed man to be taken captive by the devil, because of man's willful service to sin. But in love and in perfect harmony with God's will, Christ came to pay the price of liberation.

B. There Is Power to Deal with the Estrangement of Sin

"Your iniquities have separated you from your God; and your sins have hidden His face from you" (Isa. 59:2). The human race has been estranged by sin, but in Colossians 1:20 we read that "having made peace through the blood of His cross," Christ has "reconcile[d] all things to Himself." To effect this reconciliation, He suffered the *pain of sin*. This is something we cannot fully understand. We can only believe the fact that he was forsaken by God, so that we could be reconciled to God. Listen to his cry of dereliction on the cross: "My God, My God, why have You forsaken Me?" (Matt. 27:46).

C. There Is Power to Deal with the Punishment of Sin

"The wages of sin is death" (Rom. 6:23). And again, "The soul who sins shall die" (Ezek. 18:4). And furthermore, "When desire has conceived, it gives birth to sin; and sin, when it is full-grown, brings forth death" (James 1:15). The punishment of sin is death, but the Lord Jesus Christ has met this for us in suffering the *penalty of sin.* As a consequence, we who deserved eternal death and banishment can now be gloriously justified. "Having now been justified by His blood, we shall be saved from wrath through Him" (Rom. 5:9).

Illustration

After reading Exodus 12, a father asked one of his family why the destroyer passed over the blood-sprinkled doors of the Israelites. "Because death had been there before," his little girl quickly replied.

Similarly, if you and I have trusted Christ in all the virtue of his justifying blood, death has no more claim on us.

D. There Is Power to Deal with the Defilement of Sin

"Come now, and let us reason together," says the LORD, "Though your sins are like scarlet, they shall be as white as snow; though they are red like crimson, they shall be as wool" (Isa. 1:18). Scarlet and crimson are the hardest colors to eradicate from any fabric. So Isaiah chooses these metaphors to illustrate the measure in which sin has defiled the entire human personality. And yet, wonder of wonders, men and women can be made white as snow or wool. The supreme explanation for this is that Jesus suffered the *pollution of sin* to cleanse. "He made Him who knew no sin to be sin for us, that we might become the righteousness of God in Him" (2 Cor. 5:21). The virtue of that atoning blood answers to the defilement of sin. "The blood of Jesus Christ His Son cleanses us from all sin" (1 John 1:7).

He breaks the power of canceled sin,
He sets the prisoner free;

His blood can make the foulest clean;
His blood availed for me.

Charles Wesley (italics mine)

The third Scripture we shall examine deals with:

III. The Voice of the Blood of Christ

"And to the blood of sprinkling that *speaks* better things than that of Abel. See that you do not refuse Him who speaks" (Heb. 12:24–25). The blood of Abel cried out for vengeance. The words of God to Cain, the murderer, were: "What have you done? The voice of your brother's blood cries out to Me from the ground" (Gen. 4:10). Such a curse was pronounced on Cain that he had to exclaim, "My punishment is greater than I can bear!" (Gen. 4:13).

But the blood of Jesus speaks in more gracious tones. It articulates a message of pardon, peace, and power. Pay attention to the fact that it is "the blood of sprinkling." The *shed blood* speaks of his death at Calvary; but the *sprinkled blood* speaks of his resurrection and ascension to heaven. "But with His own blood He entered the Most Holy Place . . . having obtained eternal redemption" (Heb. 9:12). And again: "Christ has not entered the holy places made with hands, which are copies of the true, but into heaven itself, now to appear in the presence of God for us" (v. 24). So the blood of Christ is:

A. The Voice of Pardon

"In Him we have redemption through His blood, the forgiveness of sins" (Eph. 1:7). We have considered the virtue of this precious blood and how it answers to every form of sin. But the question is whether or not we know in personal experience a sense of forgiveness and pardon. Listen to the voice of the Lord: "Son [daughter], your sins are forgiven you" (Mark 2:5). "See that you do not refuse Him who speaks" (Heb. 12:25).

B. The Voice of Peace

"Having made peace through the blood of His cross" (Col. 1:20). Jesus can now say to each one of us, "Peace I leave with you, My peace I give to you; not as the world gives do I give to you" (John 14:27). And again, "Peace be with you" (John 20:19). To know this serenity and harmony of mind and heart is to be able to sing:

> Peace, perfect peace,
> In this dark world of sin?
> The blood of Jesus
> Whispers peace within.
>
> Edward Bickersteth

Illustration

A few years ago, the life of a young Arab in Mesopotamia was slowly but surely ebbing away. The white doctor bent over him in the tribal tent. Only one thing could save the youth's life, transfusion of blood from the arteries of a healthy man. The doctor, turning to the father, brothers, and cousins of the young man, asked: "From which of you may I take blood to pour into the veins of this youth and save his life?"

One and all refused to give blood, even for their own kin. The doctor saw one way to save him. Baring his own body, he poured out his blood to save the young man. The Arabs were astounded. Even the impassive Orient was deeply moved. From that day, this American missionary doctor has been able to do what he will with those Arabs, and no man dare lay a finger on him. "He is our brother now," they say. "His blood is in our veins." Jesus made peace by the blood of the cross (Col. 1:20).

Here is a peace that the world cannot give. It commences with peace *with* God on the ground of redemption, reconciliation, justification, and cleansing. It consummates in realizing the peace *of* God, amidst all the problems and pressures of daily living. "And the peace of God, which surpasses all understanding, will guard your hearts and minds through Christ Jesus" (Phil. 4:7).

C. The Voice of Power

"And they overcame him by the blood of the Lamb and by the word of their testimony, and they did not love their lives to the death" (Rev. 12:11). In this context, the devil is described as an accuser and an attacker of God's people, but in each of these approaches he is powerless against the Christian, who takes his stand on the ground of the precious blood of Christ. How can the devil accuse the conscience that has been purged by the blood of the Lamb? And furthermore, how can the devil attack a Christian who is protected by that same conquering blood? So the believer who knows the value and virtue of the blood of Christ can also know its victory.

Illustration

The story is told of Napoleon who was looking at a map of Europe. Placing his finger on Great Britain, he remarked: "Were it not for that red spot, I would have conquered the world." In like manner, the devil also looks at the map of the world. If he had his way, he would conquer the world completely; but it is a foregone conclusion that he will never do it. For there is one place on the map that symbolizes not only his utter defeat, but his eternal doom: It is the red spot marked Calvary.

Conclusion

We have considered together the value, virtue, and voice of the blood of Christ. Let us remember that the "blood of sprinkling" (Heb. 12:24) directs us to one who not only shed His blood, but rose again to sprinkle it in heaven. And as the living Lord, He wants to enter your heart and mine, to make real in us what He did for us on Calvary's cross. As He knocks and asks admission, "See that you do not refuse Him who speaks" (Heb. 12:25).

3

Radical Repentance

Luke 12:54–13:9

Unless you repent you will all likewise perish.

Luke 13:5

Introduction

The sounding forth of repentance is a lost note in gospel preaching today. For this very reason the church has been impoverished, and lost men and women have been denied the terms of God for salvation, life, and blessing. Needless to say, the doctrine of repentance is not a popular one; but, notwithstanding this, it is an evangelical as well as an unavoidable truth.

John the Baptist heralded the coming of Christ with the message of repentance. In the wilderness his voice could be heard, crying, "Repent, for the kingdom of heaven is at hand!" (Matt. 3:2). Then appeared the Savior Himself, who opened His ministry with the same message, "Repent, and believe in the gospel" (Mark 1:15). He concluded His ministry in like manner by commissioning His disciples to preach repentance and remission of sins in His name among all nations (Luke 24:47). On the day of Pentecost, Peter, in obedience to his commission, declared, "Repent, and let every one of you be baptized in the name of Jesus Christ for the remission of sins; and you shall receive the gift of the Holy Spirit" (Acts 2:38). Later Paul summed up his witness both to Jews and to Greeks in terms of "repentance toward God and faith toward our Lord Jesus Christ" (Acts 20:21). So we see that repentance is an indispensable element in our Christian gospel. In the text we have before us, there are four salient features of the call to repentance that we must consider:

I. The Truth of Repentance

"Unless you repent you will all likewise perish" (Luke 13:5). From this penetrating and searching statement of our Lord, we observe that repentance is:

A. The Divine Imperative of Salvation

"Unless you repent you will all likewise perish." A study of the word *repentance* as it is used in the Bible makes it very evident that there is no salvation apart from repentance. This does not interfere with the complementary truth that we are saved through faith. Faith alone is the instrument of justification, but justification is not the whole of salvation, and faith is not the only condition. Faith without repentance would not be the faith that leads to salvation (2 Cor. 7:10). If it is asked which comes first, faith or repentance, the answer is that they are always concurrent in operation, and therefore mutually conditioning.

In the Old Testament, the term used most frequently to denote human repentance is a word that means "to turn" or "return." The Lord says, "Turn to Me with all your heart, with fasting, with weeping, and with mourning. So rend your heart, and not your garments" (Joel 2:12–13). In the New Testament, repentance signifies "a change of mind." It consists of a radical transformation of thought, attitudes, and direction.

Illustration

> Stephen Olford relates: I like to recall in this connection an occasion during the Second World War when I was teaching the Bible to a group of soldiers. In our reading we came across this word *repentance,* and I asked someone to give me a definition. Instantly a young man stood up and said, "Do you mind, Sir, if I illustrate it?" I replied, "Go ahead." With that he marched across the room saying, "I am on my way to a lost eternity. My back is turned on God and Christ and salvation, but I hear a command from heaven saying, 'Halt, right about turn, forward march.' That, Sir, is repentance."

So we see that repentance is the divine imperative of salvation. It is also:

B. The Divine Alternative to Damnation

"Unless you repent you will all likewise perish." Without repentance we can anticipate nothing less than eternal separation from God. As we noted in our reading in Luke, the context is one of judgment. In each of the illustrations that Jesus has employed, he is emphasizing the severity of God's dealings with men and women who will not quit sin and turn to him in repentance. He points out that if we do not discern the weather aright, we will be caught in a storm or burned up in the heat; and again, if we do not settle with our adversary before the day of judgment, we will be cast into prison; and yet again, if we do not bring forth the fruits of repentance, we will be cut down like a barren fig tree (see Luke 12:54–13:9). All this adds up to our text, which says in unmistakable terms, "but unless you repent you will all likewise perish."

This, then, is the truth of repentance. Now consider:

II. The Terms of Repentance

"Unless you repent you will all likewise perish" (Luke 13:5). The two illustrations that precede our text were carefully chosen by the Lord Jesus to demonstrate with vividness and directness the terms of repentance. They are a right recognition of God and a right relationship to Him.

A. A Right Recognition of God

"Hypocrites! You can discern the face of the sky and of the earth, but how is it you do not discern this time?" (Luke 12:56). The Jews of Palestine were weather-wise. When they saw the clouds forming in the west over the Mediterranean Sea, they knew that rain was on the way. When the south wind blew from the desert, they knew that hot winds were coming. The Master's concern was that those who were wise enough to read the winds and the sky could not read the signs of the times. Or what was more important, they knew all about the wind but knew nothing about the Spirit. Their observation of the sky was accurate, but they could see nothing beyond the skies into heaven itself. They were weather-wise but spiritually blind, blind to the fact that God had visited them in the person of Jesus Christ His Son.

This is the whole significance of the two little words, "this time." There was no recognition of God in His mighty intervention in time, of His holiness and love in the life of Christ, of His redemptive purpose. Before a man can repent, he must have the right recognition of God. His whole mind and attitude must be related to the fact of God in terms of His person and purpose. There must also be:

B. A Right Relationship to God

"When you go with your adversary to the magistrate, make every effort along the way to settle with him, lest he drag you to the judge, [and] the judge deliver you" (Luke 12:58). There is only one thing to do with God, and that is get right with Him. Failure to do this involves His getting right with us at the great white throne, when, following the death sentence, we shall be banished from His presence forever. Thus the terms of repentance are clear: a right

recognition of God followed by a right relationship to God.
So I say to you:

> Get right with God, and do it now.
> Get right with God, he tells you how;
> Oh, come to Christ, who shed his blood;
> And at the cross get right with God.

E. E. Hewitt

The next important feature of repentance is:

III. The Test of Repentance

"Unless you repent you will all likewise perish" (Luke 13:5). In the parable of the fig tree, which is at the end of our text, the Savior teaches that the supreme test of repentance is *fruit*. In the language of the Gospel, these fruits are acceptance and obedience.

A. The Acceptance of Christ

"Repentance toward God and faith toward our Lord Jesus Christ" (Acts 20:21). No one has truly repented toward God unless there follows a trusting in Christ. This is what Peter meant on the day of Pentecost when he said, "Repent, and let every one of you be baptized in the name of Jesus Christ for the remission of sins; and you shall receive the gift of the Holy Spirit" (Acts 2:38).

Have you accepted the Lord Jesus Christ as your personal Savior and Lord? Have you opened the door of your heart to receive Him in all the fullness of His life and Lordship?

The further evidence of repentance is:

B. The Obedience to Christ

"Therefore bear fruits worthy of repentance" (Matt. 3:8). This could also read, "Bring forth fruits answerable to an amendment of life." Or as Weymouth puts it, "Let your lives then prove your change of heart." Williams Translation reads: "Produce, then, fruit that is consistent with the repentance you profess." These are the words of John the Baptist when he addressed his searching challenge to the people of his day. He expected nothing less than the confession of sin and holiness of life. God's test of repentance is still the same today. A person who does not forsake sin and seek to live in holiness by the power of an indwelling Spirit has never truly repented. Describing people of this kind, Jesus said, "By their fruits you will know them" (Matt. 7:20).

Have you repented? Are there fruits in your life that prove a change of heart? This leads me to the last point:

IV. The Time of Repentance

"But unless you repent you will all likewise perish" (Luke 13:5). As we have already observed, these words were spoken in a context of the urgency and uncertainty of life. Two stories are told to emphasize the unexpected day of death and doom. One concerns Galileans, whose blood Pilate had mingled with their sacrifices. This was a most unexpected event. Without warning Pilate ordered his soldiers to quell a possible revolution among the hotheaded Galileans. It happened all of a sudden, and many passed from time into eternity. Then there were the eighteen people on whom the tower of Siloam fell. Once again the catastrophe was unpredicted and sudden.

Life at best is short and uncertain. A person can perish even though Pilate never slays him. He can perish even though no tower crushes him to death. He may lie in his bed with his friends about him and even have music while he dies, but he will be damned just as surely unless he repents. In view of these solemn facts, the time for repentance is now. God says, "Behold, now is the accepted time;

behold, now is the day of salvation" (2 Cor. 6:2). The time is *now* because:

A. God's Justice Commands It

God commands "all men everywhere to repent, because He has appointed a day on which He will judge the world in righteousness by the Man whom He has ordained. He has given assurance of this to all by raising Him from the dead" (Acts 17:30–31). It is inconceivable that a moral Governor of the universe could allow such a wicked world as ours to go on indefinitely unjudged and uncleansed. A day of judgment is surely coming, and in the light of it all, men everywhere must repent. To refuse is to perish eternally.

B. God's Goodness Demands It

We read, "The goodness of God leads you to repentance" (Rom. 2:4). The goodness of God has been forever manifested in the Christ of the cross as well as the cross of the Christ. We cannot gaze on the Man of Calvary, bleeding to death, without remembering that "He was wounded for our transgressions, He was bruised for our iniquities; The chastisement for our peace was upon Him, and by His stripes we are healed" (Isa. 53:5). Indeed, there is only one response we can make to such unbounded and unmerited goodness. It is simply this:

> Love so amazing, so divine,
> Demands my soul, my life, my all.
>
> Isaac Watts

Conclusion

If men and women do not repent in the presence of such a God of love, then there can be only one alternative— eternal banishment. What is your answer to this call to repentance? To heed it is to live; to harden your heart is to perish.

Illustration

When George Whitfield preached his message of repentance in this country, as well as in Great Britain, he had many enemies who sought to oppose him. Among these was a certain Mr. Thorpe. On one occasion this man and a number of his friends decided to ridicule the great preacher. They called a meeting of supporters together and began to wager as to who could best mimic the saintly George Whitfield. With unbridled buffoonery they caused the group to rock with laughter. Last of all, Thorpe stood to his feet exclaiming, "I will beat you all." He opened his Bible and read the first text that caught his eye. The words were, "Except ye repent, ye shall all likewise perish."

Before he opened his mouth to speak, it seemed as if the Spirit of God pierced his heart with conviction so that instead of fooling and clowning, he began to say words of truth and soberness and to preach with faithfulness and fervor. The entire group was solemnized and stilled before God. The meeting broke up, and Thorpe quickly withdrew himself in great distress of soul. Several days later he found peace with God and became one of the great preachers of his day. In seeking to mock God, he had been crushed himself. In true repentance he found his way to the foot of the cross where Jesus met him in saving grace and mercy.

Let us not mock God but turn to Him in true repentance and put our faith in the Lord Jesus Christ. So shall we be gloriously saved and become the heralds of this message of life.

4

Justification by Faith

Romans 3:19–31

Being justified freely by His grace through the redemption
that is in Christ Jesus.

Romans 3:24

Introduction

In the Book of Job we are confronted with one of the fundamental questions of the ages: "How . . . can man be righteous before God?" (Job 25:4). There is a sense in which the rest of the Bible is an unfolding of the answer, but perhaps no portion of the Word of God deals with this aspect of truth more clearly and concisely than the Epistle of Paul to the Romans. The verses before us are a perfect example of this. Consider first of all:

I. The Miracle of Justification

"Being justified freely by His grace through the redemption that is in Christ Jesus" (Rom. 3:24). Let us review what Paul has been saying in this context. Employing legal language, he has declared that the sentence of the court of heaven on man is that he is a guilty sinner *without excuse:* "Every mouth . . . stopped" (v. 19). The evidence is too overwhelming for a single contrary voice to be raised. Thus man is deprived of all excuse and reduced to complete silence.

Furthermore, Paul says that man is a guilty sinner *without exception:* "All the world [is] guilty before God" (v. 19). This includes men and women individually and universally. What is more, man is a guilty sinner *without escape.*

Into this hopeless situation, however, God breaks through from heaven with a message of pardon and release for a guilty race. He announces that even though "All have sinned and fall short of the glory of God" (v. 23), there is justification free and full "through the redemption that is in Christ Jesus" (v. 24). Now this is nothing less than a miracle of grace, or unmerited favor.

A. Justification Is a Supernatural Act of Grace

"Being justified freely by His grace." There is only one Person in the universe who can act in such grace and favor; it is God himself. In fact Paul states, "It is God who justifies" (Rom. 8:33). Only the supreme Judge of the universe can declare men and women righteous who are otherwise utterly condemned. This is why Paul always sets in contrast the words *justification* and *condemnation.*

Such justification is more than forgiveness. It is complete restoration. For instance, you can forgive your child for having done wrong, and the little one can look up into your face and ask, "Am I alright now?" You reply, "Yes," but as you answer the question, the shadow has not passed from your face, and the child knows that all is not right, so he asks again, "Am I good now?" Once again you answer, "Yes," but the little fellow insists, "Then why don't you smile?" That smile spells restoration to the original relationship!

When we come to the Scriptures, we find this to be true of our position before God, for justification virtually means "being made to appear before God in a favorable light."

B. Justification Is a Saving Act of Grace

"Being justified freely by His grace through the redemption that is in Christ Jesus." Through the redemptive work of Christ, justification includes:

1. BEING SAVED FROM WRATH

"Much more then, having now been justified by His blood, we shall be saved from wrath through Him" (Rom. 5:9).

2. BEING RECKONED RIGHTEOUS

"To him who does not work but believes on Him who justifies the ungodly, his faith is accounted for righteousness" (Rom. 4:5).

3. BEING GRANTED PEACE WITH GOD

"Having been justified by faith, we have peace with God through our Lord Jesus Christ" (Rom. 5:1).

These are the saving accompaniments of being justified. The differences between the justified and the unjustified are as large as those of light and darkness, of heaven and hell. Here, then, is the miracle of justification: a supernatural and saving act of grace in which man has no part whatsoever, save that of receiving and rejoicing faith.

Illustration

Among the many biblical examples of men and women who were declared "righteous before God" is the illustrious story of a man named Noah. Read the context or tell the story and then focus on Genesis 6:8–9 with those three pungent statements concerning Noah: 1. He found grace (v. 8); 2. he was just, or righteous (v. 9); 3. he walked with God (v. 9).

But consider further:

II. The Manner of Justification

"Being justified freely by His grace through the redemption that is in Christ Jesus" (Rom. 3:24). It is important to remember that before God can extend His favor to men and women who are undone and condemned, He must vindicate himself as a just God. Thus we find in Paul's treatment of this subject that the manner of justification is carried out both propitiously and righteously. Consider this more closely:

A. God Justifies Propitiously

"Being justified freely by His grace through the redemption that is in Christ Jesus, whom God set forth to be a propitiation by His blood, through faith" (Rom. 3:24–25). The word *propitiation* denotes both an expiatory sacrifice and the idea of the mercy seat (Heb. 9:5). Scholars disagree as to which of the two meanings Paul has in mind here. I venture to suggest that both are included: the Lord Jesus is both an expiatory sacrifice and the mercy seat. Because he is the *expiatory sacrifice,* a holy God can be satisfied that every demand of His righteous law has been fully met. Because He is the *mercy seat,* guilty men can be justified. Since the blood has been sprinkled on and before the mercy seat, God can come out in grace to sinful man and pronounce him righteous on condition of his personal faith in the Lord Jesus Christ. Thus we see that on the basis of Christ's work of propitiation, God can be "just and the justifier of the one who has faith in Jesus" (Rom. 3:26). What a glorious message to guilty men!

Amplification

Propitiation underscores the conciliating elements in Christ's redemptive work: dying for man's sins (1 Peter 1:18–19); satisfying God's justice (Rom. 3:25–26); reconciling God and man (2 Cor. 5:18–19); offering the believing sinner *perfect righteousness* (2 Cor. 5:20–21).

B. God Justifies Righteously

"Being justified freely by His grace through the redemption that is in Christ Jesus, whom God set forth to be a propitiation by His blood, through faith, to demonstrate His righteousness" (Rom. 3:24–25). Because of Christ's work of propitiation, God can be righteous in declaring unrighteous man to be righteous. God justifies man judicially by His own righteous act as Judge the moment the sinner believes in Jesus as his atoning substitute.

The key word that is used to express this manner of justification is *imputation*, thus the righteousness of God is counted, reckoned, or imputed to the believer. In the same sense that our sins were laid on, or imputed, to Christ, so His righteousness is imputed to us. In other words, His death is reckoned as our death; and Paul tells us that "He who has died has been freed from sin [or justified]" (Rom. 6:7). Thus peace ensues, the curse is gone, and we are at rest. And all this is effected propitiously and righteously to the glory of God and our eternal blessing. What a gospel for you and for me!

Now let us consider how this can happen.

III. The Means of Justification

"Being justified freely by His grace through the redemption that is in Christ Jesus . . . by faith *apart from the deeds of the law* (3:24, 28, italics mine). No one can read these verses without coming to the conclusion that the means of justification are twofold. They involve repentance and faith.

A. *Repentance toward God*

"Therefore we conclude that a man is justified by faith apart from the deeds of the law" (Rom. 3:28). Paul has already declared, "All have sinned and fall short of the glory of God" (v. 23). There is no one who has kept the whole law, for James reminds us that "whoever shall keep the whole law, and yet stumble in one point, he is guilty of all" (James 2:10). Therefore if a man would be justified, he must repent of every attempt he has made to keep the law, lest he think that he can be saved by his own sinful self-efforts.

Repentance toward God is an essential means of being justified. The tax collector, of whom Jesus spoke, had reached this point when he cried, "God be merciful to me a sinner!" (Luke 18:13). And Jesus commented on such repentance, "I tell you, this man went down to his house justified" (v. 14). Tell me, have you repented of your sins and the deeds of the law? If not, will you pray this prayer?

> Not the labors of my hands
> Can fulfill Thy law's demands;
> Could my zeal no respite know,
> Could my tears forever flow,
> All for sin could not atone;
> Thou must save, and Thou alone.
>
> Augustus M. Toplady

The second means of justification is:

B. *Faith toward Christ*

"Being justified *by faith,* we have peace with God through our Lord Jesus Christ" (Rom. 5:1, italics mine). If the works of the law are voided and boasting is excluded, then man, whoever or whatever he is, must exercise simple faith if he is to receive the righteousness of God that is in Christ. Martin Luther brought to light this great doctrine of justification by faith and declared, "Justification is by grace alone, through faith alone, in Christ alone."

If you would be justified, you must believe that Jesus
died for you and that He was raised again for your justification. Such faith identifies you not only with the crucified Christ, the *ground* of your justification, but also with
the risen Lord, the *proof* of your justification. Will you then
exercise this personal faith in Christ as your Redeemer and
Justifier?

One last thought remains. It is that of:

IV. The Manifestations of Justification

"Being justified freely by His grace through the redemption that is in Christ Jesus" (Rom. 3:24). Such free and full
acquittal before the bar of God issues in certain manifestations. No one can be thus justified and fail to reveal this
experience in terms of concrete evidence. The Word of God
makes it clear that the manifestations of justification are
confession of faith and production of fruit.

A. A Confession of Faith

"By your words you will be justified" (Matt. 12:37). The
evidence of justification is a confession of faith, which is
both unquestionable and unshakable. A man's words dis-
close what is in him. "Out of the abundance of the heart
the mouth speaks" (v. 34), and thus the reality of his justification is openly confessed. This is why Paul says: "If
you confess with your mouth the Lord Jesus and believe
in your heart that God has raised Him from the dead, you
will be saved" (Rom. 10:9).

B. A Production of Fruit

"A man is justified by works, and not by faith only"
(James 2:24). Remember the words of John the Baptist
when he cried in the wilderness, "Therefore bear fruits
worthy of repentance" (Matt. 3:8). Just as *words* evidence
the confession of faith, so *works* evidence the production

of fruit. James says, "I will show you my faith by my works" (James 2:18). He is saying that faith is not faith if it produces no fruit, just as love is not love if it shows no kindness. The Bible questions any man who claims to be justified if he does not show the fruit to prove it.

Illustration

Tell again the story of the Pharisee and the tax collector in Luke 18:9–14. Why could Jesus say about the tax collector, "I tell you, this man went down to his house justified"? Carefully analyzed and applied, this makes a powerful conclusion to the sermon on justification.

Paul tells us that "Christ Jesus . . . became for us wisdom from God—and righteousness and sanctification and redemption" (1 Cor. 1:30). Therefore if we have accepted Him as our wisdom, as our righteousness (or justification), and as our sanctification, redemption must necessarily follow. Christ is not divided; justification and sanctification are inseparably bound together.

Conclusion

We have seen, then, what we mean by this glorious doctrine of justification by faith. I pray that you may know what it is to be justified as you exercise faith in Him as both your Judge and Justifier. So I bid you:

Trust the risen Christ who died,
And you will be justified—
Made to stand before God's throne,
Righteous through His grace alone.
Then live out your debt of love,
Till the hour you're called above.

S. F. O.

5

The Miracle of Conversion

Matthew 18:1–6

> Assuredly, I say to you, unless you are converted and become as little children, you will by no means enter the kingdom of heaven.

Matthew 18:3

Introduction

We believe in the miracle of conversion not only because the Bible teaches it and history exemplifies it, but especially because personal experience corroborates it. Perhaps the clearest words that were ever spoken on this subject were spoken by the Lord Jesus in this text. In these simple, but solemn words, he declared:

I. The Essentiality of Conversion

"Unless you are converted and become as little children, you will by no means enter the kingdom of heaven" (Matt. 18:3). The clear implication of this amazing statement is that everyone needs to be converted. Conversion is absolutely essential for men and women of every race, rank, or religion. There are two reasons for this:

A. By Natural Birth Man Is outside the Kingdom of Heaven

"Unless you are converted . . . you will by no means *enter* the kingdom of heaven." To be outside the kingdom of heaven is to be cut off from all that the kingdom represents, namely, righteousness, peace, and joy in the Holy Spirit. The Bible tells us that "the kingdom of God is not food and drink, but righteousness and peace and joy in the Holy Spirit" (Rom. 14:17). Just as a citizen of one country is not entitled to the privileges, the advantages, and the blessings of a foreign country, so no one who has not been born into the kingdom of God has a right to the privileges, advantages, and blessings of a heavenly kingdom.

Now this is difficult to understand outside of the teaching of the Bible. In fact in Christ's day this particular truth even puzzled a theologian by the name of Nicodemus. Jesus had to say to him, "Unless one is born again, he cannot see the kingdom of God." And again, "Unless one is born of water and the Spirit, he cannot enter the kingdom of God" (John 3:3, 5).

B. By Spiritual Birth Man Is inside the Kingdom of Heaven

"Unless you are converted . . . you will by no means *enter* the kingdom of heaven." This implies that to be converted is to enter the kingdom of heaven.

Illustration

A visitor to a country churchyard saw some unusual words engraved on one of the tombstones. The epitaph said: "Here lies an old man seven years of age." The meaning was that he had been a true Christian for only that short length of time.[1]

This involves the acceptance of the rule of God in your life and all the blessings that flow from it. Not only are there spiritual blessings, but also material benefits. "But seek first the kingdom of God and His righteousness, and all these things shall be added to you" (Matt. 6:33). So we see that everyone needs conversion, and "unless you are converted and become as little children, you will by no means enter the kingdom of heaven."

But with the essentiality of conversion, there is also:

II. The Experience of Conversion

"Unless you are converted" (Matt. 18:3); the verb *convert* is made up of the two words *com* and *vertere,* which mean "with" and "to turn." In other words, "to turn with the help of another." Conversion signifies, therefore, a transformation or a miraculous change. In terms of the New Testament, it involves:

A. *Turning to Christ*

The apostle Paul speaks of "faith toward our Lord Jesus Christ" (Acts 20:21). In personal experience, this means a commitment of your life to Christ and the full realization that in and of yourself you cannot change your character or your conduct. But once there is faith reposed in the Lord Jesus Christ, the miracle of conversion takes place.

Illustration

Some time after the sinking of the Titanic, a young man reported this story. "I am a survivor of the Titanic. When I was drifting alone that night, the tide brought a man named John Harper, from Glasgow, near me. He called out to me, 'Man, are you saved?' I replied, 'No! I am not.' He shouted, 'Believe on the Lord Jesus Christ and you will be saved.' Amazingly, when the tide took him away, it returned him to me once more. We engaged in the same brief conversation before he went down a short time later. There, alone in the night and with two miles of water beneath me, I trusted Christ. I am John Harper's last convert." Little did that struggling survivor realize that he had just entered the kingdom of heaven![2]

Perhaps the most dramatic conversion recorded in the New Testament is that of Saul of Tarsus, the archpersecutor of the early church. While on his way to haul Christians to prison and to cause them to blaspheme, he was arrested by a light from heaven. It was nothing less than the glory of the face of Jesus Christ. The moment he recognized who Jesus was and the authority of His saving call, he replied, "Lord, what do you want me to do?" (Acts 9:6). Instantly a miracle took place. Saul of Tarsus was converted and later he became Paul the apostle. On that Damascan road there was a turning to Christ and conversion followed.

B. Trusting in Christ

This is what the apostle called "faith toward our Lord Jesus Christ." In the full realization that you cannot quit sin in your own strength and that you cannot maintain the life that God expects of you without the help of another, you must trust in Christ. Lean your whole weight on Him. Commit yourself to Him who died to cleanse you by His blood, who rose to save you by His life, and who lives to keep you by His power. This then is the nature of true conversion. Our text suggests a third aspect in the miracle of conversion:

III. The Evidence of Conversion

"Unless you are converted and become as little children" (Matt. 18:3). The evidence of true conversion is becoming like little children. Let me hasten to add that this is not a call to childishness but rather to childlikeness, and there is a world of difference between these two concepts. Think, for a moment, of what a little child symbolizes.

A. The Child Symbolizes a New Beginning

Literally, the phrase "little children" means "little infant." We cannot think of a little child without accepting the concept of a new birth or a new beginning. How often we have looked into the face of a sleeping infant with the longing to start life all over again! This is what God promises to all who are truly converted, a new beginning.

B. The Child Symbolizes a New Belief

A little child is the perfect example of teachability, sincerity, and humility. In fact this is why our Lord took a little child and put him in the midst as He taught His disciples. They were vying for power and, because of their rivalry and jealousy, they were both proud and prejudiced. So Jesus said, "Become as little children."

Nobody can become a Christian without being a disciple. A disciple simply is a learner or a pupil. And the entire Christian experience is that of learning from Christ. He says, "Learn from Me, for I am gentle and lowly in heart" (Matt. 11:29). We cannot learn anything of God's good purposes for our lives without the teachability and humility that God requires. On one occasion, when surrounded by religious bigots, Jesus prayed, "I thank You, Father, Lord of heaven and earth, because You have hidden these things from the wise and prudent and have revealed them to babes" (v. 25). He teaches his secrets to those who will humble themselves and become as little children.

C. The Child Symbolizes a New Behavior

Once again the infant speaks to us of innocence, dependence, and obedience. It is the behavior that pleases God and blesses humanity. Only converted people can know the heaven-born innocence, dependence, and obedience of everyday living. This is the only standard of life that is going to clean up our churches, our homes, and our society.

Illustration

Charles Darwin visited the South Sea Islands in 1833 and thought he found subhuman evolutionary "links" in the primitive cannibals living there. Much later he returned and was astonished by the transformation in the people. The missionary work of John Paton had effected great changes. The people had been converted![3]

What our country needs is a conversion. Our sophistication and secularism have ruined us. We have forgotten how to live, how to laugh, and how to love; and these will never be recovered until we know the miracle of conversion. In fact our Savior said, "Unless you repent you will all likewise perish" (Luke 13:3). The Bible says: "Turn from your evil ways! For why should you die?" (Ezek. 33:11).

Conclusion

So we come back to our text, "Unless you are converted and become as little children, you will by no means enter the kingdom of heaven" (Matt. 18:3). Turn to Christ, trust in Christ, and know this greatest of all miracles—the miracle of conversion. And like little children praise our Savior forever.

> Hosanna, loud hosanna,
> The little children sang;
> Through pillared court and temple
> The lovely anthem rang;
> To Jesus, who had blessed them
> Close folded to his breast,
> The children sang their praises,
> The simplest and the best.
> "Hosanna in the highest!"
> That ancient song we sing,
> For Christ is our Redeemer,
> The Lord of heav'n, our King;
> O may we ever praise him
> With heart and life and voice,
> And in his blissful presence
> Eternally rejoice!
>
> Jennette Threlfall

The Overtures of the Gospel
Matthew 11:20–30

> Come to Me, all you who labor and are heavy laden, and I will give you rest. Take My yoke upon you and learn from Me, for I am gentle and lowly in heart, and you will find rest for your souls.
>
> Matthew 11:28–29

Introduction

While the episodes in Matthew 11 are not necessarily in chronological order, we have to accept the fact that the Holy Spirit has brought them together in a pattern that portrays a fourfold picture of the Lord Jesus Christ and a background to our text.

The Rebuking Christ

First of all, we have the picture of the rebuking Christ. "Woe to you, Chorazin! Woe to you, Bethsaida! For if the mighty works which were done in you had been done in Tyre and Sidon, they would have repented long ago in sackcloth and ashes" (v. 21). Jesus had moved throughout the towns of Palestine, performing mighty acts and preaching with authority and winsomeness, but the men and women of Chorazin and Bethsaida were indifferent. So the Lord Jesus had to rebuke them with stern words of indictment, judgment, and condemnation.

Illustration

A judge in India was on his way to court one day when he saw a child playing on the railroad tracks, completely oblivious to a fast approaching train. Taking his own life in his hands, the judge dashed onto the tracks and drew the child to safety just in time. However, a short time later in his courtroom, he dutifully sentenced a convicted murderer to death. In the space of a few hours this gentleman had been both savior and judge![1]

We have to remember that He who said, "Come to me, all you who labor and are heavy laden" (v. 28) is first of all the Light of lights, the God of righteousness and severity. In these words of rebuke He gives us a hint that there will be degrees of punishment in the day of judgment. For some, it is going to be more tolerable than for others.

So we have the picture of the rebuking Christ.

The Rejoicing Christ

Then there is a complete change as we are given a picture of the rejoicing Christ. "I thank You, Father, Lord of heaven and earth, because You have hidden these things from the wise and prudent and have revealed them to babes" (v. 25). There is a lilt in the voice of the Savior as He lifts up His heart in thanksgiving and praise to His Father. As a matter of fact, Luke's account tells us that Jesus "rejoiced in the Spirit" as He said this (Luke 10:21). It is one of the only occasions in the Gospels when we read that Jesus' heart actually leaped with joy!

In the inscrutable wisdom of God, the simple truths of the gospel have been hidden from the wise and prudent (that is to say, the mere intellectuals). Instead they have been revealed to babes, or those who are characterized by teachability and humility. This teaches the great truth that, whether it is a professor at the university or a little child in the home,

God's gospel levels *all* to one plane. The words come down through the centuries: "Unless you are converted and become as little children, you will by no means enter the kingdom of heaven" (Matt. 18:3).

The Revealing Christ

The third picture is that of the revealing Christ. "All things have been delivered to Me by My Father, and no one knows the Son except the Father. Nor does anyone know the Father except the Son, and he to whom the Son wills to reveal Him" (Matt. 11:27). Here is the Lord Jesus showing us that He is none other than God the Son; and that God the Father cannot be known save through Him; nor can we know the Son, unless by the Father's wonderful drawing power (John 6:44). It is an amazing revelation: He is the Creator of the universe, the King immortal, invisible, the only wise God.

The Redeeming Christ

Picture number four is the redeeming Christ. "Come to Me, all you who labor and are heavy laden, and I will give you rest. Take My yoke upon you and learn from Me, for I am gentle and lowly in heart, and you will find rest for your souls. For My yoke is easy and My burden is light" (Matt. 11:28–30). These words have brought calm, healing, and salvation to millions down through the centuries.

Here are the overtures of the gospel:

I. The Overture of the Gospel Invitation

"Come to Me, all you who labor and are heavy laden, and I will give you rest" (Matt. 11:28). Someone has rightly observed that "Jesus Christ, the Son of God, knew no greater task than to point men and women to himself." No one else in the universe has the right to do that. Notice that people are not invited to consider a policy or a program or even certain facts of doctrine, but to encounter and experience Christ.

A. Encounter Christ

"Come to Me." No word could be simpler than "come." If I were to stretch out my arms and utter that magic word to a baby, the little hands would be stretched out immediately. It is a word that is understood by the wandering boy when the mother's letter arrives with an impassioned appeal, "My son, come home. I still love you, in spite of all your rebellion and willfulness. Come!" It is understood by the doctor when the sick man cries out, "Please come, I am in need." Someone has suggested a simple acrostic to emphasize who may come to Jesus:

Children
Older people
Middle-aged
Everybody

The invitation is also to:

B. Experience Christ

"Come to Me, all you who labor and are heavy laden, and I will give you rest." There are thousands and thousands who are controlled by sin.

1. THE BONDAGE OF SIN

"You who labor." Those who are controlled by sin are continually striving to break this habit or that vice. They are shackled by sin.

2. THE BURDEN OF SIN

"And are heavy laden." Have you ever read *Pilgrim's Progress*? There is portrayed a man with a heavy burden, wending his way to Calvary's hill. Then, with one look at the cross, his heavy burden rolls away, and he cries and leaps with joy. Are you carrying such a burden? Jesus says, "Come to *Me* . . . and I will give you rest." There is magic and music in the word *rest*.

Illustration

Dr. John A. Schindler wrote a book, *How to Live 365 Days a Year.* He has proved that there is hardly a disease or complaint of our modern generation that is not due in part to emotional strain, disquiet, and *unrest.* He has tried to give a prescription, which echoes the fuller teaching of the Word of God. It is that men and women should learn tranquility, peace, and harmony.

What people need is the glorious rest that Jesus offers in our text. He gives not only spiritual peace, but physical, emotional, and mental harmony. "Peace I leave with you, My peace I give to you" (John 14:27). This is not a man-made peace, but a God-made peace procured at Calvary's cross; for there the Lord Jesus "made peace through the blood of His cross" (Col. 1:20). The rest that He offers cost His precious blood, but it is a gift that you can have now.

> My Savior, Thou has offered rest,
> Then give it now to me;
> The rest of ceasing from myself,
> To find my all in Thee.
>
> Eliza H. Hamilton

With the word of invitation, there is:

II. The Overture of the Gospel Obligation

"Take My yoke upon you" (Matt. 11:29). Remember that it is the carpenter of Nazareth who is speaking. Many a time, with His own hands He had fashioned in His father's carpentry shop yokes for the oxen. In using this metaphor, Jesus is saying two things. The obligation is to:

A. Accept a Relationship to Christ

"Take My yoke." There are many people who want to enjoy the benefits of the gospel without having a relationship to Jesus Christ. They want to know peace, pardon, power, and purpose in their lives; but mention the name of Jesus to them and they become embarrassed. They do not realize that a Christian is a "Christ's man." "He who is joined to the Lord is one spirit with Him" (1 Cor. 6:17). Are you prepared to say, "Lord Jesus, I take Your yoke on me; I stretch out my hand to meet Your pierced hand, and it will always be my joy and pride to be linked with You"?

B. Assume a Responsibility to Christ

"Take My yoke upon *you*." The yoke speaks also of service under lordship. Just as two oxen are yoked together to plough a furrow through the field, so the Lord Jesus wants to plough the furrow of life with you. In the last chapter of Mark, we read that the disciples "went out . . . *the Lord working with them* and confirming the word through the accompanying signs" (Mark 16:20, italics mine).

In this evangelistic appeal, there is not only an invitation for the heart and an obligation for the will, but also an education for the mind.

III. The Overture of the Gospel Education

A. We Are to Learn from Christ

"Learn from Me," says the Savior, "for I am gentle and lowly in heart" (Matt. 11:29). This is not merely academic knowledge; it is primarily experiential knowledge of the Savior's love. This is one of the few places in the New Testament where the heart of the Lord Jesus is mentioned. Jesus says, "I am gentle and lowly in heart." Get as close as John did. Hear the throb of Jesus' heart. Learn of His meekness. Meekness is not weakness, but strength under control. Learn of His lowliness. The word *lowly* means "close to the ground." That means "low at His feet," like Mary (Luke 10:39). Mary sat at His feet to learn.

B. We Are to Lean on Christ

"You will find rest for your souls" (Matt. 11:29). The more we learn of Christ, the more we lean on him, finding rest for our souls.

> Cast care aside, lean on thy Guide,
> His boundless mercy will provide;
> Trust, and thy trusting soul shall prove
> Christ is its life, and Christ its love.

> John S. B. Monsell

Paul puts it another way when he says: "It is no longer I who live, but Christ lives in me; and the life which I now live in the flesh I live by faith in the Son of God, who loved me and gave Himself for me" (Gal. 2:20). You know that the word *faith* just means to "lean on" or "to put your weight on."

Illustration

When John G. Paton, a New Hebrides missionary, was translating the Bible into the native tongue, he was a long time trying to find the word for "faith." One day, one of his native workers, coming in after a tiresome day, threw himself into a chair and exclaimed, "Oh, I am so tired, I must lean my whole weight on this chair." Instantly Paton cried, "Thank God, I have got my word! I have got my word!" It was the native's expression for "lean my whole weight on."[2]

Conclusion

So we find in this appeal of Jesus Christ not only an invitation to come to Him, and an obligation to take His yoke, but also an education to learn from Him increasingly so

that we may lean on Him. Will you *come, take,* and *learn?*
Look up into Christ's face and say:

> I *come,* Lord Jesus, in my need,
> Please lift sin's burden now, I plead;
> I *take* with joy your yoke of love
> and pledge to serve till called above;
> I'll *learn* of you each day, dear Lord,
> As I esteem and read your Word.

S. F. O.

The Story of Your Life

Matthew 21:33–46

A certain landowner . . . planted a vineyard. . . . And he leased it to vinedressers and went into a far country. . . . When the chief priests and Pharisees heard His parables, they perceived that He was speaking of them.

Matthew 21:33, 45

Introduction

This dramatic parable is the story of a highly favored nation that failed to realize God's great purpose for its life. As Jesus painted the word picture, He had in mind the Jews who were listening to Him, for it is recorded that "He was speaking of them." But since a nation is made up of individuals, the story is essentially one of *personal life.* The more the parable is read, the more it becomes evident that it represents the story of your life and mine. Look first of all at:

I. The Privileges of Your Life

"Hear another parable: There was a certain landowner who planted a vineyard and set a hedge around it, dug a winepress in it and built a tower. And he leased it to vine-dressers and went into a far country" (Matt. 21:33). God likens your life to a vineyard, to which He has given all his thought and care:

A. The Prevenient Care of God

He "planted a vineyard." Have you ever paused to consider the story of your coming into the world? But for God's prevenient care, you would never have been planted or born. You owe your very existence to Him. Behind your parents and secondary causes, there is the hand of your Creator. He says, "I am the LORD, your . . . Creator" (Isa. 43:15). David was quick to recognize: "You are He who took Me out of the womb. . . . I was cast upon You from birth" (Ps. 22:9–10). Medical science today has to acknowledge that physical birth is still the greatest miracle of human life. Without God's prevenient care it could never happen.

B. The Protecting Care of God

He "set a hedge around it." Perhaps you have never realized that apart from God's protecting care, you would not be alive. It is surely common knowledge to all that life from the cradle to the grave is one long battle against disease, decay, and seen and unseen forces of evil. Only when we view our lives within the context of daily dangers, can we realize the protecting care of God and say with Jeremiah, "Through the LORD's mercies we are not consumed" (Lam. 3:22).

Illustration

On Saturday, March 1, 1950, the West Side Baptist Church of Beatrice, Nebraska, was demolished by a gas-leak explosion. The time was 7:25 P.M. The choir had been scheduled to begin practice at 7:15 P.M. but by an unprecedented coincidence not one choir member arrived on time! For two sisters, the car wouldn't start. For several others, last-minute responsibilities delayed them. One lost track of the time during a conversation with a friend. Another overslept. For one reason or another every choir member was late! Surely the protecting care of God overruled that afternoon.[1]

C. The Providing Care of God

He "dug a winepress." God's goodness is such that He has provided you with a capacity to receive and recip-rocate all His good gifts. Every man is born into the world with this capacity. James 1:17 tells us, "Every good gift and every perfect gift is from above, and comes down from the Father of lights, with whom there is no variation or shadow of turning." And Paul reminds us that "God . . . gives us richly all things to enjoy" (1 Tim. 6:17). The "all things" include the temporal mercies and spiritual blessings that God has provided for our enjoyment.

D. The Preserving Care of God

He "built a tower." The tower was the lookout from which enemies within the vineyard could be detected. Here is yet another way in which God has expressed His loving care for you. He has given you an inner tower of preserving conscience to discern between good and evil. The fact that you have not heeded the inner warnings of conscience is no reflection on God's care. "That was the true Light which gives light to every man who comes into the world" (John 1:9). Here, then, are the privileges, which God has lavished on your life. Surely, as you review all these privileges, you cannot help but sing:

> When all thy mercies, O my God,
> My rising soul surveys,
> Transported with the view, I'm lost
> In wonder, love and praise.
>
> Joseph Addison

II. The Purpose of Your Life

The purpose of your life is implied in the following words: "He leased [the vineyard] to vinedressers . . . that they might receive its fruit" (Matt. 21:33–34). This suggests that when a person reaches the age of responsibility God "leases" the life for the cultivation of fruit. The fruit He expects is judgment and righteousness in the relationships of life. This seems clear from Isaiah 5, the passage from which our Lord quoted this parable. The supreme purpose of your life is to yield fruit:

A. Yield the Fruit of Spiritual Judgment and Righteousness

Bearing fruit of spiritual judgment and righteousness is rendering to God that which is justly and righteously his due. The Lord Jesus summed it up this way, "You shall love the LORD your God with all your heart, with all your soul, with all your mind, and with all your strength. This is the first commandment" (Mark 12:30). Has it ever occurred to you what that statement involves? To say the least, it means that the purpose of your life, Godward, is to yield to Him:

1. THE FRUIT OF YOUR EXPERIENTIAL LOVE

"You shall love the LORD your God with all your heart." Such love is opposed to the mere service of professionalism and nominalism. It is loving God with a heart that is regenerated and indwelt by the Holy Spirit, for "the fruit of the Spirit is love" (Gal. 5:22).

2. THE FRUIT OF YOUR EMOTIONAL LOVE

"You shall love the LORD your God with all your . . . soul." Ask yourself: Am I ashamed of being emotional over my love for God? Emotion is often demonstrated in sports, at the theater or movie, in the home, or through loving friendships. But exhibit a little emotion in your love for God and immediately it is labeled emotionalism!

3. THE FRUIT OF YOUR ENLIGHTENED LOVE

"You shall love the LORD your God with all your . . . mind." This presupposes time spent in getting to know God by studying His Word, engaging in prayer, and developing a regular church life.

4. THE FRUIT OF YOUR ENERGETIC LOVE

"You shall love the LORD your God with all your . . . strength." Many years ago a hymn was written that went like this:

> There's a work for Jesus ready at your hand,
> 'Tis a task the Master just for you has planned,
> Haste to do his bidding, yield him service true;
> There's a work for Jesus none but you can do.

> E. D. Yale

Illustration

A young boy lived with his frail mother on the fourth floor of a walk-up tenement. Out of affection for his parent, the youngster lugged many heavy buckets of coal up those flights of stairs every day. This boy's uncomplaining effort is a touching example of loving "with all his strength."[2]

Yes, God's purpose for your life is to cultivate the love of your heart, soul, mind, and strength. But having rendered Him his due, you must:

B. Yield the Fruit of Social Judgment and Righteousness

Bearing the fruit of social judgment and righteousness is rendering to men what is their just and righteous due. The Lord Jesus gave a second commandment that demands that we love our neighbor as ourselves (Mark 12:31). This means the extension of the first commandment until it affects our social life. It reflects the fact that the salvation and well-being of our fellow man is part of the fruit that God expects.

C. Yield the Fruit of Self-Judgment and Righteousness

You are to render to yourself that which is right and just. Observe the last two words of the second commandment, "You shall love your neighbor *as yourself*" (Mark 12:31, italics mine).[3] This means loving God and man with such devotion that the effect of such loving destroys selfishness, while it develops selflessness.

The story of your life is not complete without a look at:

III. The Prerogative of Your Life

"The vinedressers saw the son . . . caught him, and cast him out of the vineyard, and killed him" (Matt. 21:38–39). The most amazing thing about your life is that even though God has blessed you with privileges and purpose, you have the prerogative either to ignore Him or to acknowledge Him. How does a person ignore God?

A. By Misusing His Sovereignty

"Now when vintage-time drew near, he sent his servants to the vinedressers, that they might receive its fruit" (Matt. 21:34). In His sovereignty, God has every right to claim from your life His due; yet you have the prerogative to misuse that sovereignty by withholding a worthy and fruitful response to the love and care that He has lavished on your life.

Illustration

The story is told of the boy who lost his father while the boy was still a baby. But notwithstanding this, he was reared by a devoted mother who worked her fingers to the bone so that he might have the benefit of a university education. Things went well, and in due course he passed his examinations with distinctions. You can imagine the joy of his mother as she watched the honors that were conferred on her son. One final pleasure remained, that of embracing her son and proudly escorting him home. But as the young man filed out of the auditorium in company with others, he snubbed his mother, telling his friends that she was just "the old washerwoman who has done my laundry while I have been at university." What base ingratitude!

Undoubtedly it was such ungratefulness for God's good gifts that led Paul to say:

> Do you despise the riches of His goodness, forbearance, and longsuffering, not knowing that the goodness of God leads you to repentance? But in accordance with your hardness and your impenitent heart you are treasuring up for yourself wrath in the day of wrath and revelation of the righteous judgment of God.
>
> Romans 2:4–5

Another way we ignore God is:

B. By Abusing His Servants

We read that "the vinedressers took his servants, beat one, killed one, and stoned another" (Matt. 21:35). This abusing of God's servants is always characteristic of those who will not acknowledge the claims of God on their lives. Analyze the feelings that rise up within you when God's servants challenge your life. Enmity and hostility mean that you are beating, stoning, and killing God's servants.

Preeminently, however, you ignore God:

C. By Refusing His Son

This parable reminds us that the vinedressers "caught [the son], and cast him out of the vineyard, and killed him." This is the greatest sin that anyone can commit, for it virtually means crucifying the Son of God again, and putting "Him to an open shame" (Heb. 6:6).

> Matchless grace! Amazing story—
> "I will send My only Son."
> And the Lord Himself His glory
> Veiled, and came, the lowly One,
> And Creation donned her mourning,
> Filled with wonderment to see
> Man his mighty Maker spurned
> Slaying him upon a tree.
>
> A. Naismith[4]

Is it any wonder that the story concludes with the destruction of those who perpetrate such a crime as the murder of the Son of God? Think again of the privileges and the high purpose of your life. Surely such considerations demand the right choice.

Conclusion

Recognize God's sovereignty by yielding to Him the fruit of your life. Let the language of your heart be:

> Love so amazing, so divine,
> Demands my soul, my life, my all.
>
> Isaac Watts

Salvation for a Call

Romans 10:11–17

For whoever calls upon the name of the LORD shall be saved.

Romans 10:13

Introduction

Paul is addressing readers who were experts at complicating what was otherwise explicit and clear. The Jews could see no salvation outside of certain religious ceremonies and human effort. Paul, however, argues such ideas out of court and declares that God's salvation may be experienced only on the principle of simple faith in Christ. In verse 10 the apostle has already spoken of the faith that believes and the faith that confesses. Now he invites the faith that calls. He says, "Whoever calls upon the name of the LORD shall be saved." "But why call?" asked someone. The answer is because of:

I. The Urgency of Salvation

The main idea implicit in the word *call* suggests urgency. For example:

A. The Urgency of Distance

The word *call* signifies "to make an appeal," as when Paul declares before Festus, "I appeal to Caesar" (Acts 25:11). Therefore to call on the name of the Lord is virtually to confess your distance from God and to appeal to Him for mercy. "But your iniquities have separated you from your God; and your sins have hidden His face from you, so that He will not hear" (Isa. 59:2). Is it any wonder that we have to call? The only redeeming feature about it is that, while we are at a distance from God, He is never distant from us. Paul tells men "that they should seek the Lord, in the hope that they might grope for Him and find Him, though He is not far from each one of us" (Acts 17:27).

The call also suggests:

B. The Urgency of Distress

The words of our text also occur in Joel 2:32 and Acts 2:21. On each occasion they are used in a context of distress because of God's impending judgments against sin. Both Joel and Peter see "the great and [awesome] day of the LORD" (Acts 2:20), and against this background they proclaim that "whoever calls on the name of the LORD shall be saved." How relevant to the present hour is the message contained in our text. "All the world may become guilty before God" (Rom. 3:19 KJV). "He who does not believe the Son shall not see life, but the wrath of God abides on him" (John 3:36).

We must not deceive ourselves by the false securities of shallow optimism, nor must we foolishly rebel against the fear-creating contemplations of God's judgments. The Bible appeals to the emotion of fear, as well as of love, and declares, "The fear of the LORD is the beginning of knowledge" (Prov. 1:7). Some men, alas, will never call for mercy until they see their plight as God describes it. What, then, do those words really mean: "All the world may become guilty"? It is the picture of guilty humanity sitting in the condemned cell because of God's wrath against sin, with the sword of judgment hanging perilously overhead. How long before that sword will fall is known to God alone. All we know for sure is that the only chance to call on the name of the Lord is *now!*

Illustration

There is a village in Switzerland located on the slope of a great mountain, directly beneath an enormous outcropping of rock. Over the ages the massive crag has become separated from the main bulk of the mountain by great fissures that slowly widen year by year. Were that rocky cliff to plunge down, it would sweep away the village and its population to utter destruction. Engineers have repeatedly warned the people of their imminent danger. The villagers have been offered aid to move away to safety yet they live on in their doomed dwellings. They reassure themselves with the thought that, "Things may last our lifetime and— even longer."[1]

No one can realize the seriousness of this picture without sending out the distress signal, the call for mercy.

The call of faith further suggests:

C. The Urgency of Decision

This is the vital sense in which Paul uses the word *call.* He has been directing the thoughts of his readers to a definite, urgent, and personal trust in Christ. His assurance is that "Whoever believes on Him [the Lord Jesus] will not be put to shame" (Rom. 10:11), will not be disappointed. Then he urges, "Whoever calls upon the name of the LORD shall be saved" (v. 13).

Have you ever sounded out this call of distance, distress, and decision? The urgency of salvation indicates that you should call now, without any further delay.

You ask again, why salvation for a call? The answer is because of:

II. The Uniqueness of Salvation

"[Call] upon the name of the LORD" (10:13). The uniqueness of God's salvation is comprehended in the fact that it is available on terms that are simple enough for anyone. After all, it does not involve very much to call on the name of a fireman, but to do so is to have an entire fire service ready to assist you. It does not involve very much to call on the name of a policeman, but to do so is to have the full authority of civil law on your side. It does not involve very much to call on the name of a physician, but to do so is to have all the value of medical knowledge related to your need. In the same way, to "call upon the name of the LORD" is to set in motion the greatest saving force in the universe.

The name of the Lord in Joel 2:32 is "Lord" or simply "Savior." It is the name that *heralds* the Savior's miraculous birth: "And [Mary] shall bring forth a Son, and you shall call His name JESUS, for He will save His people from their sins" (Matt. 1:21). It is the name that *marks* the Savior's exemplary life: He is known as "Jesus of Nazareth" (Mark 16:6). It is the name that *represents* the Savior's atoning death: "THIS IS JESUS, THE KING OF THE JEWS" (Matt. 27:37). It is the name that *declares* the Savior's triumphant resurrection: "You seek Jesus of Nazareth, who was crucified. He is risen!" (Mark 16:6). It is the name that *announces* the Savior's glorious return: "This same Jesus . . . will so come" (Acts 1:11). And, most wonderful of all, it is the name that *proclaims* the Savior's uniqueness to save: "Nor is there salvation in any other, for there is no other name under heaven given among men by which we must be saved" (Acts 4:12). To call on that name, therefore, is to acknowledge the significance of Jesus Christ, to honor the throne of the universe, to receive the favor of God, and to realize the power of the gospel for salvation—to every one that believes.

Illustration

J. Wilbur Chapman tells us that at the close of a battle in the days of World War I, a young man was found lying on the battlefield. A soldier stopped to help him. The dying man said, "My father is a man of large wealth in Detroit. If I have strength, I will write him a note, and he will repay you for this kindness." And this is the letter he wrote: "Dear Father, the bearer of this letter made my last moments easier and helped me to die. Receive him and help him, for Charlie's sake."

The war ended, and the soldier sought out the father in Detroit. The unimpressive appearance of the man caused the father to ask him to leave his place of business. "But," said the stranger, "I have a note for you, in which you will be interested." He handed him the little, soiled piece of paper. When the wealthy man's eyes fell on the handwriting and name of his son, all was instantly changed. He threw his arms about the soldier, drew him close to his heart, and put at his disposal everything that wealth could provide. It was the son's name that made the difference!

If you want the welcoming arms of God thrown around you and you desire to experience the uniqueness of His salvation, then call on the name of the Lord. Within the salvation of that name you will find:

A. The Forgiveness of Christ

"To Him all the prophets witness that, through His name, whoever believes in Him will receive remission of sins" (Acts 10:43).

B. The Favor of Christ

"And whatever you ask in My name, that I will do, that the Father may be glorified in the Son" (John 14:13).

C. The Fellowship of Christ

"For where two or three are gathered together in My name, I am there in the midst of them" (Matt. 18:20). See that you do not fail to call on the name of the Lord and be saved.

Once more you ask: Why salvation for a call?

III. The Universality of Salvation

"Whoever calls" (Rom. 10:13). That word *whoever* proclaims that God's salvation is universally available. The call of faith can be echoed by man:

A. Wherever He Is

In every country: "For God so loved the world" (John 3:16).

B. Whoever He Is

For every color: "Go into all the world and preach the gospel to every creature" (Mark 16:15).

> Red and yellow, black and white,
> All are precious in his sight.
>
> Edwin L. Bowyer

C. Whatever He Is

For every class: "For there is no partiality with God" (Rom. 2:11). Rich or poor, learned or unlearned, great or small, old or young, good or bad: All may come. The "whoever" of God's universal salvation includes you. See that

you do not exclude yourself through failing to read your
name into the "whoever."

Illustration

I'm so glad that the verse does not say: "If Stephen Olford
calls on the name of the Lord," for if that were so, no one else
could be saved. "Whoever" means "everybody."

A London street Arab defined the word "whoever" as: "Let
'em all come!"

A dying young man said, "Mother, put my finger on 'Whoever,'" and then he passed from death to life.

Conclusion

So we have seen that God's salvation is *universal*. Therefore make your call *personally*. We have seen that God's
salvation is *unique*. Therefore make your call *believingly*.
We have seen that God's salvation is *urgent*. Therefore make
your call *immediately*. Let the language of your heart be:

> O God, I pray your favor—
> As at your Throne I plead;
> I name your Son as Savior,
> And "call" in all my need.

S. F. O.

The Fears That Keep Us from Christ

Luke 8:26–39

They were seized with great fear.

Luke 8:37

Introduction

The miraculous deliverance of the demoniac of Gadara is told by Matthew, Mark, and Luke. The story is one of tragedy turned to victory, a case history of a man who was possessed by such demonic forces that he was too strong to tame, too crude to clothe, and too vocal to silence. Mark 5:5 tells us that "night and day, he was in the mountains and in the tombs, crying out and cutting himself with stones."

What man could not do, however, Jesus performed with consummate compassion and gentle majesty. So miraculous was the transformation that when the news reached the city, the people hurried to find the demoniac "sitting at the feet of Jesus, clothed and in his right mind" (Luke 8:35). The legion of demons that had once possessed him were ordered to leave the demented man and enter a herd of swine, which "ran violently down the steep place into the lake and drowned. When those who fed them saw what had happened, they fled and told it in the city and in the country . . . for they were seized with great fear" (vv. 33–34, 37). The fears that made the Gadarenes beg Jesus to leave their region are similar to those that keep people from Jesus Christ today. What are they?

I. The Fear of the Supernatural

"They were seized with great fear" (Luke 8:37). Something miraculous had taken place, and this always causes people to fear. If this reaction of awe is a genuinely repentant fear, it results in salvation; if it is a rebellious fear, it results in judgment. When the apostle Paul defines the two aspects of God's awe-inspiring character in Romans 11:22, he speaks of it as "the goodness and severity of God." Character is the outshining of God's supernatural nature. This is precisely what these Gadarenes saw on that memorable day.

A. There Was the Supernaturalism of the Grace of God

When Legion saw Jesus, he "fell down before Him" (Luke 8:28). Mark tells us that he "worshiped Him" (Mark 5:6). Here was a man who broke chains and terrified an entire city, yet in the presence of the Lord Jesus, he was a worshiper. The lion had become a lamb. Nothing can effect such change apart from the supernatural grace of God (Titus 2:11).

Illustration

The supernaturalism of God's grace is nowhere better personalized than in the life story of the author of the legendary hymn "Amazing Grace." In the corner of the churchyard of the fourteenth century Church of Saints Peter and Paul in Olney, England, that story is summarized by the hymnist's tombstone: "John Newton, Clerk; once an infidel and libertine, a servant of slaves in Africa, was by the rich mercy of our Lord and Saviour Jesus Christ preserved, restored, pardoned, and appointed to preach the faith he had long labored to destroy."[1]

Amazingly, some people are so seared by their sins or else satisfied in their sins that they are afraid of the grace of God. When men and women despise, ignore, or object to such evangelical terms as *grace, faith,* and *salvation,* they are in trouble.

B. There Was the Supernaturalism of the Wrath of God

The spokesman for the demons cried with a loud voice, "What have I to do with You, Jesus, Son of the Most High God? I beg You, do not torment me!" (Luke 8:28). People may mock the thought of judgment and hell, but the demons do not! Here was a man possessed by so many demons that he called himself Legion. In the time of Christ, a Roman legion contained six thousand foot soldiers and three hundred horses. Here the name was evidently used to express the number and force of the demonic powers that held sway over this man's entire personality. But in the presence of Jesus, the demons realized their ultimate destiny and begged the Master not to send them "into the abyss." It is the same Greek term employed five times in the book of Revelation for the "bottomless pit" (Rev. 20:3). With this in mind, you can imagine how the herdsmen felt when, with one word of command, the entire herd of swine, now possessed of demons, "ran violently down the steep place into the lake and drowned" (Luke 8:33).

Once again, this is one of the fears Satan uses to keep men and women from Christ. He characterizes God as a God of judgment but he fails to point out that before He is a God of judgment, He is a God of grace. Only when grace is spurned does God judge man. When a man prefers to cling to his sin in preference to Christ, then he must suffer the consequences of death, judgment, and hell (Rom. 6:23; Ezek. 18:4; Heb. 9:27).

Illustration

One of the greatest paintings of all time is Michelangelo's "The Last Judgment." The action of the painting centers on Christ as he raises his arm in a gesture of damnation. The painting pictures the dead as they are resurrected to be judged. As hell releases its captives, the judge of heaven reviews their works. The entire painting reflects the despair of that generation. When the painting was unveiled, a storm of conviction fell on the viewers. All Europe trembled.[2]

Is the fear of the supernatural holding you back from Christ? If so, let me tell you that "God is love" (1 John 4:16), and "there is no fear in love; but perfect love casts out fear, because fear involves torment" (v. 18).

II. The Fear of the Sensational

"They were seized with great fear" (Luke 8:37). Scholars believe that Gadara was a small township where life was normally quiet. For years nothing had happened on that hillside where pigs were fed each day, except for the rantings and mutilations of the demoniac. Suddenly all was changed; something sensational had taken place.

A. There Was the Sensational Activity of the Master

"He . . . commanded the unclean spirit to come out of the man" (Luke 8:29). Time and again the townspeople had tried to tame this demoniac, but he had broken his bonds in pieces and had become a menace to the community. Banished from town, he lived in the tombs, crying out night and day and slashing himself with stones. But on this day, One called Jesus commanded the unclean spirit to come out of the man.

If you stop and think about it, people today crave sensationalism in every area of life, except that of the spiritual. An evangelistic crusade is written off as "mass hysteria." An altar full of seeking souls is described as "religious emotionalism." Thus many people are kept from Jesus Christ because of His sensational effect. Because He is supernatural, however, He has to be sensational. When a miracle ceases to be sensational, it is no longer a miracle.

B. There Was the Sensational Publicity of the Master

"When those who fed [the pigs] saw what had happened, they fled and told it in the city and in the country. . . . Then the whole . . . surrounding region of the Gadarenes asked Him to depart from them, for they were seized with great fear" (Luke 8:34, 37). Jesus Christ can never be hidden. His light shines into every area of life. In fact the very nature of deity is that of self-disclosure. This is the meaning of creation, history, revelation, and redemption.

It is important to observe that when the delivered man sought to remain with Jesus, the Master instructed him, "Return to your own house, and tell what great things God has done for you. And he went his way and proclaimed throughout the whole city what great things Jesus had done for him" (v. 39). One reason why people do not commit themselves to Christ is because it means confessing Christ. But this is how it should be. Romans 9:33 declares, "Whoever believes on Him will not be put to shame." One day Jesus Christ is going to be glorified and verified before an entire universe. Every being in heaven, on earth, and under the earth will "confess that Jesus Christ is Lord, to the glory of God the Father" (Phil. 2:11).

III. The Fear of the Sacrificial

"They were seized with great fear" (Luke 8:37). We cannot examine this story without observing that the events of that day involved moral as well as material costliness.

A. The Moral Costliness

"The herd ran violently down the steep place into the lake and drowned" (Luke 8:33). It is not too far-fetched to assume that the reason demonic powers prevailed in that area of the country was because of the corrupt business of the Gadarenes. To traffic in swine was a breach of the Mosaic Law (see Leviticus 11:7). If the Gadarenes were Jews, and there seems strong reason for supposing they were, they were habitually sinning. The Bible declares, "Righteousness exalts a nation, but sin is a reproach to any people" (Prov. 14:34).

What is true of a nation is also true of a city. When God breaks into a situation, sin has to go. This is moral costliness. Are we prepared to pay the sacrifice of getting right with God? The Bible says, "If we confess our sins, He is faithful and just to forgive us our sins and to cleanse us from all unrighteousness" (1 John 1:9).

B. The Material Costliness

"Then the demons went out of the man and entered the swine" (Luke 8:33). Why did our Lord allow the demons to go into the herd of swine and thus destroy them? In the Bible we see God continually taking away animal life to teach spiritual truth, as in the case of the Old Testament sacrifices. In addition, God destroyed these pigs to demonstrate His displeasure with the Gadarenes for keeping them. Getting right with God may often involve material costliness for ourselves and others. Christians often have to give up jobs because they are incompatible with their new life in Christ. But God is no man's debtor. Anything we give up for Christ, God will more than repay.

What is keeping you back from Christ? Is it fear? How can slavish fear be replaced with saving faith? The answer is in our story. Verse 28 tells us that "when [the man] saw Jesus, he cried out [and] fell down before Him." Even though this poor renegade was tormented by the demons indwelling him, so that it was difficult to tell who was speaking and who was acting, the response to Christ was all that mattered.

1. THERE WAS A SENSITIVITY TO CHRIST

"When he saw Jesus." Even in his depraved state he was aware of Jesus among those tombs. Unseen to natural eyes but real to faith, the Lord Jesus is standing right now at the door of your life. He says, "If anyone hears My voice and opens the door, I will come in to him and dine with him, and he with Me" (Rev. 3:20).

2. THERE WAS A SUBMISSION TO CHRIST

"He . . . fell down before Him." Are you ready to yield mind, heart, and will to the sovereignty of Christ as Lord and Savior? The Bible says, "If you confess with your mouth the Lord Jesus and believe in your heart that God has raised Him from the dead, you will be saved" (Rom. 10:9). Remember, "No one can say that Jesus is Lord except by the Holy Spirit" (1 Cor. 12:3).

3. THERE WAS A SUPPLICATION TO CHRIST

"He cried out." No cry to the Savior ever goes unanswered. Romans 10:13 tells us, "Whoever calls upon the name of the Lord shall be saved." He who died on Calvary's cross and rose from the dead now sits enthroned at the right hand of the throne of God. There He sits to hear the cry of any sinner, under any circumstances. If repentance and faith are real, He hears the cry and by His Spirit comes to indwell the heart and life.

Conclusion

Do not let fears keep you back from Christ. On the contrary, allow the Spirit of God to replace those slavish fears by faith in the only One who can set you free.

"Rabbi! begone! Thy powers
Bring loss to us and ours;
Our ways are not as Thine—
Thou lovest man—we, swine.
Oh get Thee gone, Omnipotence, and take this fool of Thine!
His soul? What care we for his soul? Since we have lost our
    swine."
Then Christ went sadly: He had wrought for them a sign
Of love and tenderness divine—
They wanted swine!
Christ stands without your door and gently knocks,
But if your gold or swine the entrance blocks,
He forces no man's hold, He will depart
And leave you to the treasures of your heart.

                                    John Oxenham (italics mine)[3]

10

The Indwelt Life

Colossians 1:25–29

Christ in you, the hope of glory.

Colossians 1:27

Introduction

The genius of Christianity is what might be termed "the indwelt life." This means that Christianity is not the attempt of sinful and failing man to copy the historic Christ who lived two thousand years ago, nor the moral endeavor of mere humans to live up to the Sermon on the Mount. On the contrary, Christianity is Christ—living His life in and through your personality and mind. It is not so much a question of the *imitation* of Christ as the *impartation* of Christ. This is what the apostle Paul means when he speaks of "Christ in you, the hope of glory." To help us understand what is meant by this glorious concept of the indwelt life, observe three things:

I. The Miracle of Christ's Incoming

"Christ in you, the hope of glory." Even though we speak so simply of receiving the Lord Jesus into our heart and life, we must never forget that His incoming constitutes one of the greatest mysteries and miracles in the universe. In describing this experience, the apostle had to search for words in his attempt to convey what he calls the mystery or secret of Christ's indwelling. It is plain from the New Testament that Jesus Christ can enter the human heart only by a miracle:

A. A Miraculous Operation

To the Ephesian believers Paul could say, "For this reason I bow my knees to the Father of our Lord Jesus Christ. . . . that He would grant you, according to the riches of His glory, to be strengthened with might through His Spirit in the inner man, that Christ may dwell in your hearts through faith" (Eph. 3:14, 16–17). We need the miraculous operation of the Holy Spirit to strengthen our inner man to say yes to the incoming and indwelling of Christ. The devil does not want this to happen, unbelieving friends do not wish the miracle to take place, and what is worse, our own perverse natures are hostile to the incoming of Christ. This is why Jesus has to stand outside the door of our hearts and patiently and persistently knock. Listen again to his words, "Behold, I stand at the door and knock. If anyone hears My voice and opens the door, I will come in to him and dine with him, and he with Me" (Rev. 3:20).

Not only is there a need for a miraculous operation, but also a miraculous revelation.

B. A Miraculous Revelation

The Savior says, "*Behold,* I stand at the door, and knock." Until our eyes are open to see Him as redeemer, master, and friend, we will never desire to have Him in our life. Furthermore, it takes a miraculous revelation to make Jesus real in our life after He actually comes in. The apostle Paul put it this way, "When it pleased God . . . to reveal His Son in me" (Gal. 1:15–16). Such a revelation was not only miraculous, but utterly transforming and compelling. I cannot possibly tell you of the wonder, the glory, and the unspeakable joy that comes when Jesus steps into the life of a man, a woman, a boy, or a girl. This, then, is the first thing I want you to notice. The second is:

II. The Measure of Christ's Indwelling

"Christ in you, the hope of glory" (Col. 1:27). It is not without significance that Paul uses the title *Christ,* rather than the name *Jesus.* The term *Christ* means Messiah, or anointed one. The idea of anointing, furthermore, is always related in Scripture to the threefold office of prophet, priest, and king. The implications of this truth are tremendous. What God is saying to us is simply this, that the measure of Christ's indwelling in our lives must be recognized in terms of his being our teacher, savior, and master.

A. *Christ as Teacher*

In his office as prophet, He has been sent by God to man to teach us all we must know about the Father. So Jesus says to each one of us, "Learn from Me, for I am gentle and lowly in heart, and you will find rest for your souls" (Matt. 11:29). And again, "If you abide in My word, you are My disciples indeed. And you shall know the truth, and the truth shall make you free" (John 8:31–32). As the indwelling Christ, He is our teacher, and He expects us to hear, heed, and honor His word.

B. *Christ as Savior*

As priest, He represents the saving work of God for each one of us. The Bible tells us, "If when we were enemies we were reconciled to God through the death of His Son, much more, having been reconciled, we shall be saved by His life" (Rom. 5:10); and, "Therefore He is also able to save to the uttermost those who come to God through Him, since He ever lives to make intercession for them" (Heb. 7:25). As indwelling savior, He is saving us moment by moment. This is the secret of victory over sin, self, and Satan. Can anything be more wonderful than to know this saving life of Christ?

C. Christ as Master

As king, Jesus claims undisputed sway and mastery in our lives. Listen to these words: "For to this end Christ died and rose and lived again, that He might be Lord" (Rom. 14:9); and, "But sanctify the Lord God in your hearts, and always be ready to give a defense to everyone who asks you a reason for the hope that is in you" (1 Peter 3:15). The measure of His indwelling must be nothing less than King of Kings and Lord of Lords in our lives. If these terms are met, then there follows what is our concluding thought:

III. The Ministry of His Infilling

"Christ in you, the hope of glory" (Col. 1:27). If Jesus Christ is truly teacher, savior, and master in your life, then all that is meant by the phrase "the hope of glory" becomes an indwelling bright reality. Your life, then, is filled with hope and glory. The New Testament reveals that this life of hope and glory means at least three things:

A. Life Is Filled with Certainty

"This hope we have as an anchor of the soul, both sure and steadfast" (Heb. 6:19). In a day of pessimism, uncertainty, and fear, what a joy it is to be filled with certainty and assurance! The Christian is not a pessimist or an optimist, but a realist. This is what gives him confidence in a world filled with uncertainty.

Amplification

Read 2 Peter 1:16–21 and tell the story again of the Savior's presence and glory on the Mount of Transfiguration and then amplify the points of certainty concerning the reality of Christ in our lives. It is a historic reality (vv. 16–18). It is prophetic reality (vv. 19–20). It is a dynamic reality (v. 21) through the work and power of the Spirit.

B. Life Is Filled with Radiancy

In his letter to Titus, Paul refers to this hope of glory as "the blessed hope" (2:13). The Christian does not look for death or even for heaven. His hope is in the coming again of the Lord Jesus Christ. No one can read the New Testament documents without being confronted with the inescapable truth of the second advent. We are told that this same Jesus, who indwells us by His Spirit now, is to return again personally, physically, and gloriously. That day will consummate all the joys and longings of every genuine believer. The hope of this event is spoken of in the Bible as a "joy inexpressible and full of glory" (1 Peter 1:8).

C. Life Is Filled with Purity

"Everyone who has this hope in Him purifies himself, just as He is pure" (1 John 3:3). The infilling of Christ through the work of the Holy Spirit is the supreme secret of a life of purity and victory. It is quite impossible for anyone to live a life of holiness and triumph in this world without the dynamic of an indwelling Lord. Temptation and tribulation are far too strong for any human being, but when Jesus comes into the life, all is changed. This is what Paul means when he says, "I can do all things through Christ who strengthens me" (Phil. 4:13).

Illustration

The story is told of an ailing man who lived alone in a drab and dirty little house. A Christian worker visited him and led him to Christ. This visit was followed by several oth-

ers with gifts of food and one glorious plant that seemed
to light up his humble home. Immediately the old man start-
ed to *clean up* his dwelling place.

In a similar way, no one can live a dirty life with a *pure*
Christ dwelling within!

Conclusion

So we have seen something of the wonder and glory of
this indwelt life. We have touched on the miracle of Christ's
incoming, the measure of His indwelling, and the ministry
of His infilling. Do you know this indwelt life? Can you
say, "Christ in me, the hope of glory"? If not, are you prepared to seek the Holy Spirit's enabling?—first, to see Jesus,
and then to ask Him to come into your heart and life. Then,
and only then, can you pray:

> Lord, my heart is open,
> Enter now, I pray;
> Every barrier's broken,
> You must have *full sway!*

> S. F. O.

Guarded by God

1 Peter 1:1–9

> Kept by the power of God through faith for salvation ready to be revealed in the last time.
>
> 1 Peter 1:5

Introduction

How often we have heard a person say, "I want to be a Christian but I am afraid I will not be able to keep it up!" Needless to say, all such notions are the result of satanic brainwashing. Christianity is not something we "keep up." Christianity is a glorious Person who saves and keeps us. That Person is none other than the all-powerful Son of God. Nobody knew this better than Peter, who had often failed his Lord but at last learned the lesson to distrust himself and only trust his Savior. And so he opens his Epistle with one of the most delightful doxologies we find in the New Testament (see verse 3). As somebody has said, "We find in this introduction to his first epistle the Te Deum, sung to the remembrance of the redeeming grace of God." Peter's central theme in this doxology is the keeping power of God. Let us then consider:

I. The Purpose to Which We Are Kept

"Kept by the power of God through faith for salvation." Once we understand that God has a purpose to which He is saving His people, the adequacy of His keeping power is never questioned again. Let us remember that God commits Himself to finish what He begins. Paul states this with no uncertain language in the opening verses of his Epistle to the Philippians, "Being confident of this very thing, that He who has begun a good work in you will complete it until the day of Jesus Christ" (Phil. 1:6). To read a statement like this and to have any doubt as to the ultimate purpose of God in our salvation is nothing less than unconscious blasphemy. Now Peter speaks in our text of being "kept by the power of God through faith for salvation." An examination of the context reveals that the writer had at least three thoughts in mind when defining this great word *salvation.* Included in the range of God's saving grace we have:

A. An Initial Transformation

"Blessed be the God and Father of our Lord Jesus Christ, who according to His abundant mercy has begotten us again" (1 Peter 1:3). More literally, this would read "begotten us anew." This is where salvation begins. It involves a new birth. This is one of the unique phrases of the Christian's vocabulary, which is not found in other religions. Other systems emphasize culture, training, discipline, education, and evolution, but not the new birth. Christianity begins not with turning over a new leaf, but with taking on a new life. Another translation of this text reads as follows: "God has given to us a new life" (Twentieth Century). Now here is a life that has no end. It is described in the

New Testament as eternal and everlasting, so that even though it begins on earth, it goes on forever in heaven.

Illustration

Tell simply and meaningfully the story of the Master's encounter with Nicodemus (John 3:1–16). Here was a scholar and *the* teacher of the Old Testament and yet he was blind in sin (v. 3), bound in sin (v. 5), and born in sin (v. 6). He needed the miracle of the new birth, and so does every member of the human family.

But with this initial transformation there is also:

B. A Continual Expectation

"Begotten . . . again to a living hope through the resurrection of Jesus Christ from the dead" (1 Peter 1:3); again, the Twentieth Century version renders this "a new life of undying hope." Before regeneration there was no hope, but once a person is born again he is given a living and undying hope. It is interesting to observe that the hope here is associated with the resurrection of Christ, and this is quite understandable. Paul says, "If Christ is not risen, your faith is futile; you are still in your sins!" (1 Cor. 15:17). Because Jesus is alive, there is now a hope that nothing can dim. The grave is no longer a terminus, but a thoroughfare.

This expectation is part of the process of salvation. That is why Paul speaks of being "saved in this hope" (Rom. 8:24). We all know the experience of anticipating some great event or the arrival of some beloved relative or friend, and part of being saved is being sustained by this expectation of eternal life. So in this word *salvation* we have an initial transformation, a continual expectation, and then:

C. An Eternal Consummation

"To an inheritance incorruptible and undefiled and that does not fade away, reserved in heaven for you" (1 Peter 1:4); salvation is not only past and present, but also future. This is one of the most glorious concepts of

our Christian gospel, and the point that Peter is making
here is that God is keeping us for this impending consummation. It includes, first, a consummating deliverance. The phrase, "for salvation ready to be revealed in the
last time" (v. 5), is full of significance. It gathers up into
itself not only the completion of our deliverance from
sin, but also the redemption of our bodies and our personal presentation in the presence of the Father with
exceeding joy. No wonder Peter uses the words, "salvation
ready to be revealed in the last time."

But with the consummation of our deliverance, there is
also the consummation of our inheritance. There is a sense
in which God has given us an inheritance here on earth.
Paul speaks of Christ "in whom also we have obtained an
inheritance" (Eph. 1:11). That inheritance constitutes all
the spiritual blessings in heavenly places in Christ. However, there is also a future inheritance, and Peter describes
this as "an inheritance incorruptible and undefiled and
that does not fade away, reserved in heaven."

To Peter's readers, who had already lost their part in
Israel's earthly inheritance, this thought of the sure inheritance of heaven would give great comfort and compen-
sation. No people were more persecuted than the Hebrew
Christians to whom he was writing. They were deprived
of homes, possessions, and even life itself. But the Spirit of God makes it clear that privations here on earth are
not to be compared with what awaits us in terms of our
home and estate in heaven. It is an inheritance incorruptible (or indestructible), undefiled (or unstained),
that fadeth not away (or kept fresh in color), and reserved
for us (or kept under watch).

No human mind or heart can conceive what God is
holding in store for those who are His children, and
therefore heirs.

So we see that those who trust Jesus Christ are kept
for a purpose. It is just inconceivable that God should
fall short of all His purpose in salvation for those He has
begotten to this "living hope."

Do you know anything of this initial transformation? Have you been born again? Are you being saved daily by the expectation of the gospel? Have you the assurance of that final consummation, when God's full deliverance and inheritance are made your very own? The purpose of God's keeping power is to bring you through to the fulfillment of this wonderful purpose.

Now let us think of:

II. The Power in Which We Are Kept

"Kept by the power of God" (1 Peter 1:5); scholars point out that this should read, "kept *in* the power of God." The reason for this is not difficult to ascertain. The whole idea behind this word *kept* is that of being guarded or surrounded. It is a military term and is used again and again in the New Testament in such a context. For instance, we read, "In Damascus the governor . . . was guarding the city . . . with a garrison" (2 Cor. 11:32). And then Paul uses it when he writes of "the peace of God, which surpasses all understanding, will guard your hearts and minds through Christ Jesus" (Phil. 4:7). This is a picture of some defenseless position or some unwalled village out in the open, with a strong force around it through which no assailant can break and in the midst of which the weakest person can sit secure.

This idea suggests a number of scriptural passages, both in the Old and New Testaments. Let us recall one or two. "The name of the Lord is a strong tower; the righteous run to it and are safe" (Prov. 18:10). And again, "He who dwells in the secret place of the Most High shall abide under the shadow of the Almighty" (Ps. 91:1). When we come to the New Testament, we have to list only the scores of verses in which the believer is found "in Christ," and we are satisfied. To be in Christ is to be utterly secure. Paul puts it beautifully when he says, "For . . . your life is hidden with Christ in God" (Col. 3:3). To be thus in Christ is to be well guarded:

A. Guarded from the World

"In the world you will have tribulation; but be of good cheer, I have overcome the world" (John 16:33). The world is a cruel and hostile place. The sooner we recognize that the world system is not only non-Christian, but thoroughly anti-Christian, the sooner we will take shelter in our Lord Jesus Christ. This is why James says that "friendship with the world is enmity with God" (James 4:4). John tells us, "All that is in the world . . . is not of the Father" (1 John 2:16). Therefore, if we are to know preservation while we walk this pilgrim pathway, we must learn what it is to abide in Christ. Jesus prayed not that we should be taken out of the world, but kept in the world (John 17:15). This means guarded behind the battlements of some great fort, and those bulwarks and battlements represent no one else but our Lord Jesus Christ. He said, "In the world you will have tribulation; but . . . I have overcome the world" (John 16:33). How wonderful to be at peace in the midst of a noisy, warring, and distracting world!

Illustration

Stephen Olford recounts: When I was a boy, living in the heart of Africa with my missionary parents, there were occasions when we camped in very dangerous areas, surrounded by wild beasts and hostile tribes. There was only one way to remain safe and secure, especially at night. It was to light and *maintain* log fires all around the campsite. As long as these fires blazed, man and beast were kept away. In a similar but even more wonderful way, "The angel of the LORD *encamps all around* those who fear Him, and delivers them" (Ps. 34:7, italics mine).

B. Guarded from the Flesh

"So then, those who are in the flesh cannot please God. But you are not in the flesh but in the Spirit, if indeed the Spirit of God dwells in you" (Rom. 8:8–9). To be in the Spirit is to be in Christ, and Paul tells us, "If Christ is in you, the body is dead because of sin, but the Spirit is life"

(Rom. 8:10). If the world is the external foe, the flesh is the internal foe. The uncrucified flesh life provides the bridges for the world and the flesh to make their incursions into the human personality. That is why the apostle describes the triumphant Christian as a man or a woman who has "crucified the flesh with its passions and desires" (Gal. 5:24). To abide in Christ by the power of the indwelling Spirit is to know constant victory over the flesh. This is what Paul means when he says: "Therefore, brethren, we are debtors—not to the flesh, to live according to the flesh. For if you live according to the flesh you will die; but if by the Spirit you put to death the deeds of the body, you will live" (Rom. 8:12–13). What a wonderful provision God has made against the onslaughts of the flesh! Oh to know this moment-by-moment protection from the subtle attacks of the flesh life!

C. Guarded from the Devil

Addressing His Father, Jesus said, "I do not pray that You should take them out of the world, but that You should keep them from the evil one. . . . as You, Father, are in Me, and I in You; that they also may be one in Us" (John 17:15, 21). To be in Christ is to know complete victory over the devil, for at Calvary He wonderfully overcame him. We read that on the cross He "disarmed principalities and powers, He made a public spectacle of them, triumphing over them in it" (Col. 2:15). And again, He overcame "him who had the power of death, that is, the devil" (Heb. 2:14). Therefore we ought to be able to say with the apostle, "We are more than conquerors through Him who loved us" (Rom. 8:37).

Here, then, is the keeping power of our God, not only from the external world and the internal flesh, but also from the infernal devil. To be in Christ is glorious victory. How can anyone hold back from being a Christian on the grounds of being afraid of slipping or falling? In the light of this mighty power, surely we ought to believe what the Bible says when it states so clearly that He "is able to keep you from stumbling, and to present you faultless before the presence of His glory with exceeding joy" (Jude 24).

So we have seen the purpose to which we are kept and the power in which we are kept. Now look at:

III. The Process by Which We Are Kept

"Who are kept by the power of God through faith for salvation" (1 Peter 1:5); in His matchless wisdom God has not devised some complicated means by which we should experience this keeping power. In utter simplicity He says we are kept through faith, and this is nothing less than the Christian's response to God's provision. If God could save us without faith, He would most certainly do it, but He does not because He cannot. As we have already said, faith is simply our response to His provision. There is nothing arbitrary about it. If we do not exercise faith, we cannot have what He offers. Just as you must open the window to let in the fresh air and pull up the blind to let in the light and take in food to be nourished, so you must exercise faith to know the power of God in your life. In simple words:

A. You Must Take Christ by Faith

Faith involves acceptance of a person. "As many as received Him, to them He gave the right to become children of God, to those who believe in His name" (John 1:12). Until you receive Christ, you are not in Christ; and until you are in Christ, you cannot be kept by the power of God. As A. B. Simpson used to put it, "You take; God undertakes." When you take Him as your life, you live. When you take Him as your power, you last.

B. You Must Trust Christ by Faith

The essential meaning of faith is trust. When the Bible speaks of exercising faith it is really exhorting each one of us to "Trust in the LORD with all [our] heart; and [to] lean not on [our] own understanding" (Prov. 3:5). So faith is trust in a person. For you to trust Christ implicitly and completely you must, first of all, learn the utter unreliability of self-trust. True faith must always be measured by self-despair; or in other words, the measure of your trust in Christ must be the measure of your distrust in self. So to know this keeping power of God you must agree to say:

> Simply trusting every day,
> Trusting through a stormy way;
> Even when my faith is small,
> Trusting Jesus, that is all.
>
> Edgar P. Stites

C. You Must Thank Christ by Faith

Trustful faith is thankful faith. Jesus put it beautifully when He said, "Whatever you ask . . . believing, you will receive" (Matt. 21:22). Faith is not only asking for something, but it is thanking God for what He has already given. Surely this is the sentiment of the great apostle when he says at the conclusion of one of his finest treatments of the resurrection triumph of Christ: "Thanks be to God, who gives us the victory through our Lord Jesus Christ" (1 Cor. 15:57).

If we want to live in Christ, walk in Christ, and fight in Christ, then there must be taking faith, trusting faith, and thanking faith. This is exactly what Paul means when he says, "I live by faith" (Gal. 2:20); "we walk by faith" (2 Cor. 5:7); and "fight the good fight of faith" (1 Tim. 6:12).

If we have truly taken Christ to be our life and trust Him moment by moment, then we should thank Him for His keeping power. According to His promise, we are guarded from the world, from the flesh, and from the devil until His final purpose of salvation is gloriously realized. What a life of triumph and satisfaction for all who will accept it! How often do you deliberately and consciously sit down and reflect on God's protecting grace, and then say, "Thank you, Lord"?

Conclusion

So we have seen the purpose in which we are kept, the power in which we are kept, and the process by which we are kept. What hinders you, then, to be a Christian? If you want to know what it is to be guarded by God, then take Christ, trust Christ, and thank Christ.

12

Spiritual Unpreparedness

Matthew 25:1–13

Then the kingdom of heaven shall be likened to ten virgins
who took their lamps and went out to meet the bridegroom.
Now five of them were wise, and five were foolish.

Matthew 25:1–2

Introduction

Woven into this familiar Eastern wedding scene is the truth
of the certain return of the Lord Jesus Christ. He came to
earth to win His bride, the church; but in this story we see
Him coming back to take His bride to Himself. And for this
advent He bids us watch and be ready. He uses this parable to illustrate the nature of spiritual unpreparedness.
With the story before us, therefore, let me draw your attention to three vital facts about spiritual unpreparedness.

I. It Is a Fashionable Way of Life

"Then the kingdom of heaven shall be likened to ten virgins" (Matt. 25:1). Never was a statement more true of Christendom, for if ever there was a mixture of prepared and unprepared, of wise and foolish in the church, it is today. Indeed, it is fashionable to be numbered among God's people without a true experience of spiritual preparedness. Even Horatio Bonar in his day had to declare: "I looked for the church and I found it in the world; I looked for the world and I found it in the church." The ten young women are spoken of as having:

A. *A Common Profession*

"Ten virgins . . . took their lamps" (Matt. 25:1). They *all* took their lamps. The emphasis here is on the outward rather than on the inward. It was the fashionable thing to carry what we might call the symbol of religious profession. Indeed, the devil has scored one of his greatest advantages against Christianity on this very point. He is perfectly satisfied when the fashionable thing is for people to look like Christians without being Christians.

B. *A Common Intention*

They "went out to meet the bridegroom" (Matt. 25:1). Their profession was the same and so was their intention. But even with their set intention, the remarkable thing is that five of them never questioned their *fitness* to meet the bridegroom. These are the religious people of today whose moral lives appear to be beautiful. It seems that they have been good all their days, and because of this they have never questioned their condition before God. There is a great difference between mother-of-pearl and soap bubbles. Similarly, it is quite possible to have many beautiful points of resemblance to the true Christian life and yet be destitute of the real secret of spiritual value and enduring power.

Illustration

There was a king of England called Ethelred who was never ready to meet his enemies. He had to always try to buy them off. He earned the nickname "Ethelred the Unready." In his reign, enemies like the Danes made many successful invasions of his land.[1]

In like manner, spiritual unpreparedness, though well-meaning, will only bring defeat and heartache. As long as people appear to have profession and intention in their religious life, they seem to be content.

Have you been caught up into the fashion? If so, beware, because:

II. It Is a Foolish Way of Life

"Those who were foolish took their lamps and took no oil with them" (Matt. 25:3). The foolish never test their spiritual experience by the ultimate crises of life. One crisis may mean the coming again of Jesus Christ; another may mean death. The question is, How does your spiritual experience react to these crises? The Bible always declares foolish the man who is unprepared to meet his God. He may be a rationalistic man, but God says, "The fool has said in his heart, 'There is no God'" (Ps. 14:1). He may be a materialistic man, but God says: "You fool! This night your soul will be required of you; then whose will those things be which you have provided?" (Luke 12:20). He may be a religious man, but God says, "Those who were foolish took their lamps and took no oil with them." When the crisis came, those foolish virgins discovered two disillusioning facts:

A. They Were Unprepared to Meet the Bridegroom

"And the foolish said to the wise, 'Give us some of your oil'" (Matt. 25:8). During a lifetime, it is a simple matter to move along with the fashion of religion and live as it were by proxy, but when the final crisis comes, only personal experience counts. "Give us some of your oil," they cried, for they had no oil themselves. In the Bible, oil in the vessel is suggestive of the Holy Spirit. Paul reminds us that "If anyone does not have the Spirit of Christ, he is not His" (Rom. 8:9). No mortal can give to another that which will fit him for heaven. And yet such an experience of the indwelling Spirit is the guarantee of fitness for Christ's coming and heaven.

Illustration

John was the chauffeur of a Christian whom God had prospered. The Christian often witnessed to his driver. One day as he urged the claims of Christ on the chauffeur, the believer spoke of the coming of the Lord and the sad result if a person was not saved at His return. "John, when the Lord Jesus comes you may have my cars. You and your wife may come and live in my house and enjoy ownership of all that I possess."

That night, overwhelmed with joy, the driver told his wife of their good fortune. Later, however, he realized the implications of his master's offer. At midnight John loudly knocked at his master's door. The Christian was startled to see his driver at such a late hour. "Oh sir, I don't want your cars, your property, or your money! I want to be saved, sir. I want to be ready, like you, for the coming of the Lord."[2]

The other disillusioning fact was:

B. They Were Unable to Meet the Bridegroom

"Our lamps are going out" (Matt. 25:8) was their sad wail. Instead of thrilling with the joy of the bridegroom's coming, they were in a state of utter darkness, doubt, and distress. Foolish are the people who never test their spiritual experience by the ultimate crises of life. Does the fact of the coming again of Jesus Christ confirm your personal experience of the indwelling Spirit and the assurance of a returning Savior? If not, you are a fool because:

III. It Is a Fatal Way of Life

"The door was shut" (Matt. 25:10). Today the door of grace stands open wide to receive the Bridegroom and His bride. But there is coming an unpredictable, sudden, and decisive moment when the door is going to be closed. When that happens, all the spiritually unprepared will be damned. This means:

A. A Lost Hope

"The door was shut." All hope was lost. No amount of knocking would ever gain them admission. The door of sovereign grace cannot be opened or shut by the human hand. When it is closed, it is finally closed.

Illustration

A lady who heard George Whitefield in Scotland preach on these words, "The door was shut," witnessed two young men in the audience laugh off the solemn truth. One said to the other in a jocular undertone, "Well, what if the door is shut? Another will open."

Mr. Whitefield proceeded further with his sermon then suddenly remarked, "Maybe there is some careless trifling person here today who would ward off the force of this impressive subject by lightly thinking, 'What matter if the door is shut? Another will open.'" The two young men looked at each other as if paralyzed. Whitefield continued, "Yes, another door *will* open, and I will tell you what door it will be: it will be the door into the bottomless pit, the door of hell!—the door that conceals from the eyes of angels the horrors of the damned."

B. A Lost Soul

The bridegroom answered and said, "Assuredly, I say to you, I do not know you" (Matt. 25:12). What devastating and chilling words! But they were deserved. These virgins had had as much time to prepare as those who went into the marriage with the bridegroom but they preferred to be foolish and fashionable, and so they lost their

hope and their souls. For them and for all others who
follow their train, it will mean eternal hell.

No wonder the Lord closes this story with that impassioned warning, "Watch therefore, for you know neither
the day nor the hour" (v. 13). Everything culminates in that
final word *watch*. What did He mean by "watching"?
Did He mean that you are forever to be talking about the
coming of the Bridegroom and forming your convictions
that He is coming? No, the ten virgins did that! What is
it then to watch? Without doubt, it means to see to it that
you have that mystic oil of the Holy Spirit in your life.
We have seen already that "if anyone does not have the
Spirit of Christ, he is not His" (Rom. 8:9). The question
is, How can you receive the Spirit of God into your life?
The answer to that question is clearly and simply summed
up in the closing words of Peter's sermon on the day of
Pentecost, "Then Peter said to them, 'Repent, and let every
one of you be baptized in the name of Jesus Christ for
the remission of sins; and you shall receive the gift of the
Holy Spirit'" (Acts 2:38).

Conclusion

Stated in three very simple words, the conditions for
receiving the Holy Spirit into your life are:

1. *Turn.* "Repent." This involves turning your back on
   sin, the old life, and the old direction and facing up
   to God with His new life, new direction, and holiness.
2. *Trust.* "Be baptized." Baptism is the outward expression of an inward experience. In baptism a person
   testifies that he or she has put his or her trust in the
   Lord Jesus Christ.
3. *Take.* "You shall receive the gift of the Holy Spirit."
   If you have turned to God and trusted in Christ, then

the Word exhorts you to receive the Holy Spirit; receive Him as the Father's gift, receive Him as a person, receive Him as the One who guarantees your spiritual preparedness for time and eternity. Will you turn, trust, and take? Only then will your life be prepared and purified for the coming of the heavenly Bridegroom.

13

Man's Priceless Treasure

Mark 8:34–38

For what will it profit a man if he gains the whole world, and loses his own soul?

Mark 8:36

Introduction

We live in an age of devaluation. The most precious things of life, to an alarming extent, have lost their old-time worth. Our civilization has become increasingly materialistic in its objects, ideas, and values. This materialism, open or disguised, is the inevitable consequence of thinking that above and beyond this world there is nothing more. And what else can we expect when some of our own scientists tell us that they cannot distinguish between economic and spiritual values? Indeed, Professor J. B. S. Holdane has stated that in his opinion "the realization of economic values was the prerequisite to the realization of spiritual values." In plain words he advocates that we make the acquisition of material gain our primary objective in life and leave spiritual things to take care of themselves!

To those who know their Bible, however, it will become apparent at once that such a philosophy of life is the very opposite of the teaching of our Lord who said, "Seek first the kingdom of God and His righteousness, and all these things shall be added to you" (Matt. 6:33). Notwithstanding this categorical statement by the Master, men and women have been so successfully brainwashed that they have forgotten that the most priceless treasure that they possess is the *soul*.

How important it is, therefore, that we should take time to reexamine what the Lord Jesus had to say about man's priceless treasure. No doubt, you will have noticed from our reading that when Jesus faced men and women with this question of the soul, He mixed no terms. He simply declared, "What will it profit a man if he gains the whole world, and loses his own soul? Or what will a man give in exchange for his soul?" (Mark 8:36–37).

You may rightly inquire then, "What is the soul of man?" The biblical answer to that question is that the soul is that invisible, immortal, and rational part of our being that distinguishes us from brute creation and makes us resemble our Maker. The soul is the sum of those faculties within us that makes us conscious of our existence. The soul actuates, directs, or disposes in all the relations of our lives. The soul is that treasure in us that never dies, but lives on eternally in one of two places, heaven or hell: in heaven, if in God's keeping; in hell, if in the devil's keeping.

So as we consider this subject in light of our text, I pray that God will reveal to you what is your solemn responsibility with regard to your soul. Let us observe, then, that the first thought in our text is:

I. The Preciousness of the Soul

"What will it profit a man if he gains the whole world?" (Mark 8:36). The preciousness of the soul may be assessed by:

A. Humanity's Estimate of the Soul

It is a fact of human history that thinking men of every nation, however barbarous, have always recognized that the soul outlives, and therefore more than transcends, the value of the material world. Consider the philosophy of these thinkers:

1. CYRUS

Cyrus (600–529 B.C.), who was educated in the schools of one of the most illustrious Persian sages, declared, "I cannot imagine that the soul only lives while it remains in this mortal body."

2. SOCRATES

Socrates (470–399 B.C.), the prince of Greek philosophers, in his last hour said to his judges, "We are about to part. I am going to die; you are going to live. Which of us goes the better way is known to God alone."

3. STERNE

Laurence Sterne (1713–1768), the British humorist and brilliant intellect, when asked about the human soul, exclaimed, "I am positive that I have a soul: nor can all the books with which the materialists have pestered the world ever convince me to the contrary."

The soul of man, therefore, is more precious than anything in the world. If man loses his soul, he loses all.

B. Hell's Estimate of the Soul

The devil knows the soul of man is precious. This is why he blinds men's eyes to everything but materialism, which damns the soul. The Bible reminds us that, "If our gospel is veiled, it is veiled to those who are perishing, whose minds the god of this age has blinded, who do not believe, lest the light of the gospel of the glory

of Christ, who is the image of God, should shine on them"
(2 Cor. 4:3–4).

C. Heaven's Estimate of the Soul

1. THE FATHER GOD

God, who made all the worlds and all that is in them,
when He estimated the preciousness of a human soul,
did not think in terms of the millions of rolling spheres
within the universe, nor of the glory of the heavenly
host. Instead, He looked on His only and well-beloved
Son and said, My Son is the value of precious souls.
"For God so loved the world that He gave His only
begotten Son, that whoever believes in Him should not
perish but have everlasting life" (John 3:16).

2. THE LORD JESUS

In perfect agreement with God's estimate of the soul,
Jesus gave His all to redeem men's souls. So Peter
reminds us, "You were not redeemed with corruptible things, like silver or gold . . . but with the precious
blood of Christ" (1 Peter 1:18–19).

3. THE HOLY SPIRIT

The Holy Spirit has one supreme ministry in the
world: to convince men and women of the true sense
of value in relation to their soul. Speaking of the Spirit's ministry, Jesus said, "When He has come, He will
convict the world of sin, and of righteousness, and of
judgment" (John 16:8). You may ask, Why of sin, righteousness, and judgment? The answer is of sin, because
sin is the curse of the soul; of righteousness, because
righteousness is the cure of the soul; of judgment,
because judgment is the condemnation of the soul.

4. THE CHRISTIAN CHURCH

The church has always highly prized the preciousness of the soul. Consider the record of men and

women who have been burned, shot, hounded, and hanged simply because they sought the salvation of immortal souls.

Illustration

Stephen Olford relates: A missionary in this category will ever live in my memory. He had come home from the infested forests of the Congo Basin with the only surviving member of his little family, a baby girl of eighteen months. I had the privilege of hearing this dear man tell of his work among the Pygmies of Africa.

After the meeting, I invited him to supper. As we talked, I became awed and humbled as I learned of the cost that he had to pay to reach those precious Pygmies. He told me that during the first year of their term on the field, his wife and he had lost their little boy. Sorrowfully, they laid the body to rest, took courage from their God, and pressed on with the work. Then arrived a baby girl to gladden their home; but hardly had this happy event taken place when his beloved wife contracted a dread fever. For days the missionary fought for her life without avail. Finally she passed away in his arms, whispering with her last breath, "Darling, don't give up!" Without another human soul to share his tears, he buried the precious remains alongside the grave of his little boy.

As he told his story, I noticed a look of pain steal across his face. I asked if I could help in any way. "No," he replied, "I have filaria, and the doctor can do nothing for me." "My dear man," I exclaimed, "how can you think of returning to the field with a baby daughter in Wales and your body in this condition?" The look that the missionary gave me has never ceased to haunt me. Bursting into tears, he cried, "Brother Olford, have you no heart for the precious souls of Pygmies in Central Africa? Do you realize that as far as I know, there is no other missionary working amongst them?"

I want to tell you, I never slept that night. Instead, I spent the hours on my knees crying to God to teach me the value of the human soul.

But as precious as the human soul is, our text speaks of:

II. The Perdition of the Soul

"What will it profit a man if he . . . loses his own soul?" (Mark 8:36). With all the preciousness of the soul, man can lead it into eternal perdition through:

A. Spoiling the Soul by the World

We are warned to "abstain from fleshly lusts which war against the soul" (1 Peter 2:11). And John reminds us that all that is in the world is "the lust of the flesh, the lust of the eyes, and the pride of life" (1 John 2:16). Nothing scars and defiles the soul more than these fleshly lusts. And until your soul is in the safe keeping of Jesus, you are wide open to every attack the world can make.

B. Selling the Soul to the World

The Bible tells us, "Buy the truth, and do not sell it" (Prov. 23:23), and yet, like Esau, men and women are selling their birthright for what amounts to a passing meal, when compared with eternal values (Heb. 12:16–17). The New Testament is also full of illustrations of people who sold their soul to the world:

1. THE RICH YOUNG RULER

This young man faced the alternatives of gold and God (Mark 10:17–22). The Savior told him, "Sell whatever you have and give to the poor, and you will have treasure in heaven; and come, take up the cross, and follow Me" (v. 21). That was the issue for this man. But he favored gold instead of God "and went away grieved" (v. 22). He sold his soul for possessions.

2. HEROD THE KING

Herod lived in the praise of men (Acts 12:20–23). And it happened that on a certain day he arrayed himself in royal apparel and sat on his throne and made an oration to the people. And the fickle crowd gave a shout saying it was the voice of a god and not of man.

And the sacred record tells us that "immediately an angel of the Lord struck him [Herod], because he did not give glory to God. And he was eaten by worms and died" (v. 23). Herod sold his soul for popularity.

3. PONTIUS PILATE

Pilate (John 19:12–16) tried to save the Lord Jesus from death by crucifixion until he heard the people cry, "If you let this Man go, you are not Caesar's friend" (v. 12). From that moment he played into the hands of the crowd in spite of every assurance he had of the innocence of Jesus. Pilate sold his soul for power.

4. FELIX THE GOVERNOR

Governor Felix (Acts 24:24–27) had trembled under the fearless preaching of Paul the apostle; but "wanting to do the Jews a favor, left Paul bound" (v. 27). In spite of being exposed by the searchlight of God's Word concerning his unrighteousness, his intemperance, and his injustice, he chose to continue in a life of sin. Felix sold his soul for pleasure.

As a servant of the Lord, I want to ask you: For what price are you selling your soul? Is it for worldly possessions or popularity or power or pleasures? Remember that Esau could not buy back his birthright, even though he sought it with tears and repentance.

There's a line that is drawn by rejecting our Lord,
Where the call of his Spirit is lost,
And you hurry along with the pleasure-mad throng—
Have you counted, have you counted the cost?
Have you counted the cost, if your soul should be lost,
Tho' you gain the whole world for your own?
Even now it may be that the line you have crossed,
Have you counted, have you counted the cost?

A. J. Hodge

C. Starving the Soul in the World

"How shall we escape if we neglect so great a salvation?" (Heb. 2:3). Neglecting or refusing the means of God's saving grace starves the soul. We are told that Charles Darwin, in the evening of his life, confessed that he had starved his soul. Is it not tragic to think of the thousands of men and women who starve their souls daily amidst the plenteous provision of a land like this? What home has no Bible or access to a religious program on radio or TV? What locality has no church with a faithful ministry? What man or woman has the slightest excuse in an enlightened age like ours? God have mercy on us and save our souls today!

III. The Preservation of the Soul

Jesus declared, "Whoever loses his life for My sake and the gospel's will save it" (Mark 8:35). In other words, to preserve the soul eternally, man must lose it *in Christ.* "O but to lose my soul in Christ," says someone, "is to lose my identity." We reply that nothing could be further from the truth. To lose your soul in Christ is to find complete individuality: For only in Christ is the personality truly integrated, for "you are complete in Him" (Col. 2:10). Furthermore, to lose your soul in Christ is to have the personality reoriented, or preserved blameless. So the apostle prays, "May your whole spirit, soul, and body be preserved blameless at the coming of our Lord Jesus Christ" (1 Thess. 5:23).

The vital question that now arises is, How may you preserve your soul in Christ? Jesus made this clear in the following words, "Whoever desires to come after Me, let him deny himself, and take up his cross, and follow Me" (Mark 8:34). Here are the conditions of Christ and His gospel. You must:

A. Deny for Christ

"Whoever desires to come after Me, let him deny himself." This means the renunciation of anything and every-

thing that would hinder your coming to Christ. Think of
that dramatic story of blind Bartimaeus. The opportunity of a lifetime had come, for Jesus had bidden the beg-
gar to come to Him for healing. And we read that "throw-
ing aside his garment, he [Bartimaeus] rose and came to
Jesus" (Mark 10:50). There was nothing intrinsically
wrong with that garment! Many a cold day it had kept
the blind man warm. But at this point in his life, it could
have hindered his coming to Christ; so he cast it aside.
Indeed, he sacrificed the good for the better, the better
for the best. Nothing was going to impede his advance
to the only One in the world who could heal and save
him.

Are you prepared to do this? Are you prepared to cast
away anything that would hold you back from trusting
Jesus now? Come, cast aside that fear, that prejudice, that
pride and rise and follow Christ.

B. Decide for Christ

"Let him . . . take up his cross." To the would-be fol-
lower of Jesus, the cross represents shame, suffering, sacrifice, and ultimately perfect salvation in Christ. To take
up that cross means personal faith in the Christ of that
cross. To be identified with Him is to die to self and sin
and to live to righteousness and God. To live to righteousness and God is to have your soul saved and preserved. So take up that cross. Let the language of your
heart be:

> I take, O cross, thy shadow
> For my abiding place;
> I ask no other sunshine than
> The sunshine of His face;
> Content to let the world go by,
> To know no gain or loss,
> My sinful self my only shame,
> My glory all the cross.
>
> Elizabeth C. Clephane

C. Dare for Christ

"Let him . . . follow Me." Dare to follow Christ in life or in death, for the glory of God alone.

Conclusion

Only in response to such denying, deciding, and daring faith can God eternally save and preserve your soul. So I ask:

> Will you deny for Christ,
> And let him have full sway?
> Will you decide for Christ,
> And dare to walk his way?
> Then give your answer here and now,
> As low before his cross you bow.

S. F. O.

Notes

Chapter 1: *Saved by Grace through Faith*

1. A. Naismith, *1200 Notes, Quotes, and Anecdotes* (Chicago: Moody, 1962), 66.
2. Ibid., 2.
3. Walter Baxendale, *Dictionary of Illustrations for Pulpit and Platform* (Chicago: Moody, 1949), 221, adapted.

Chapter 2: *The Blood of Christ*

1. Paul Lee Tan, *Encyclopedia of 7700 Illustrations* (Dallas: Bible Communications, Inc., 1979), 208, used by permission.

Chapter 5: *The Miracle of Conversion*

1. Baxendale, *Dictionary of Illustrations*, 413, adapted.
2. Naismith, *1200 Notes*, 45.
3. Tan, *Encyclopedia of 7700 Illustrations*, 395, used by permission.

Chapter 6: *The Overtures of the Gospel*

1. Naismith, *1200 Notes*, 108, adapted.
2. Ibid., 66.

Chapter 7: *The Story of Your Life*

1. Tan, *Encyclopedia of 7700 Illustrations*, 512, adapted, used by permission.
2. Ibid., 763, adapted, used by permission.
3. It is important to point out that there are not three commandments. The last two words of the second commandment are an extension of the inclusiveness of God-given love.
4. Naismith, *1200 Notes*, 122.

Chapter 8: *Salvation for a Call*

1. Baxendale, *Dictionary of Illustrations,* 182, adapted.

Chapter 9: *The Fears That Keep Us from Christ*

1. The Billy Graham Team, *Crusader Hymns and Hymn Stories* (Chicago, Ill.: Hope Publishing, 1967), 7–8, adapted.
2. George Sweeting, *Who Said That?* (Chicago: Moody, 1995), 283, adapted.
3. John Oxenham, quoted in Naismith, *1200 Notes,* 201.

Chapter 12: *Spiritual Unpreparedness*

1. Naismith, *1200 Notes,* 166, used by permission.
2. Ibid., 34, adapted.

Stephen F. Olford has served as a pastor in England and America and is also an international speaker and radio/TV personality. His Stephen Olford Center for Biblical Preaching in Memphis provides ongoing training in biblical preaching as well as resources for preachers. Dr. Olford is the author of numerous books.

Stephen Olford Center for Biblical Preaching

Our History

The Institute for Biblical Preaching was founded in 1980 to promote biblical preaching and practical training for pastors, evangelists, and lay leaders. After fifty years of pastoral and global ministry, Dr. Olford believes that the ultimate answer to the problems of every age is the anointed expository preaching of God's inerrant Word. Such preaching must be restored to the contemporary pulpit!

The Stephen Olford Center for Biblical Preaching was dedicated on June 4, 1988, in Memphis, Tennessee. It is the international headquarters for Encounter Ministries, Inc., and houses the Institute for Biblical Preaching.

Our Strategy

The purpose of the Institute for Biblical Preaching is to equip and encourage pastors and laymen in expository preaching and exemplary living, to the end that the church will be revived and the world will be reached with the saving Word of Christ. The program includes four basic activities:

- Institutes on expository preaching, pastoral leadership, essentials of evangelism, the fullness of the Holy Spirit, the reality of revival, and other related subjects.
- Workshops for pastors and laymen to preach "live" in order to have their sermons, skills, and styles critiqued constructively.
- 1-Day Video Institutes on Anointed Biblical Preaching hosted around the country for pastors and laymen who invite us.
- Consultations on pastoral and practical matters.

For further information write Encounter Ministries, P.O. Box 757800, Memphis, TN 38175-7800; call (901) 757-7977; fax (901) 757-1372; e-mail Olford@memphisonline.com; or visit our World Wide Web site at www.olford.org.